10-4-2016

Dad,

    To another father who
raised children with a
foundation of family & faith.

            Love,

                Sherry

Happy Birthday!

RAISING BOYS THE ZELLER WAY

BY STEVE & LORRI ZELLER
PARENTS OF LUKE, TYLER, AND CODY
WITH STEPHEN COPELAND

RAISING BOYS THE ZELLER WAY

Visit the website at **www.zellerbook.com** *or*

Follow us on Twitter and Facebook:

twitter.com/zellerbook

facebook.com/RaisingBoysTheZellerWay

Published by The Core Media Group, Inc., P.O. Box 2037, Indian Trail, NC 28079.

Cover Design: informdesign.us
Interior Design: Nadia Guy
Front Cover Images: University of Notre Dame, University of North Carolina, and Indiana University
Back Cover Image: Sandy Clarke Photography
Additional Images: Provided by Steve and Lorri Zeller

"I really enjoyed getting to know Steve and Lorri during my time as a coach at Butler University. Every time that we spoke, I felt like they brought great perspective to being parents of such high-achieving children, on and off the court. Theirs is an incredible story of a faithful, tight-knit family—a family that had a unique impact on a state that is crazy about hoops."

Brad Stevens, Boston Celtics head coach and former Butler University head men's basketball coach

"In this book, Steve and Lorri encapsulate what it means to sincerely want to raise up young men who have a foundation of family and faith that will sustain them throughout their lives. Hopefully it will impact those who read it as they apply the many truths in this book."

Bobby Jones, 1983 NBA champion, eight-time NBA All-Defensive First Team

"Getting to know Steve, Lorri, Luke, Tyler, and Cody Zeller has truly been one of the highlights of my life. I coached Tyler for four years and felt extremely fortunate every day. I should have recruited Luke and I did recruit Cody (and was extremely saddened when he didn't come to UNC) and every occasion with that family was a joy. Steve and Lorri should be THE role model for parenting in today's basketball culture. How pleasant they made my life!"

Roy Williams, University of North Carolina men's basketball coach

"Honesty and humor throughout the book, and the do's and don'ts of parenting (learned through mistakes) make this a great book for sports and non-sports fans alike, but especially for those who enjoy basketball. There isn't a story as unique as this one, where the family opens up about raising three boys who would each earn Indiana Mr. Basketball, total six State championship rings between them, each play Division I basketball at major programs, and all earn NBA contracts. Most importantly, they are boys of integrity and faith."

Brett Honeycutt, managing editor of Sports Spectrum magazine

"Steve and Lorri Zeller raised three terrific basketball players, but more importantly, three tremendous young men. As parents, they were engaged in all aspects of their sons' lives. How they could keep track of everything, I don't know, but they did. This book is insightful for all parents, especially those who have children playing sports."

Mike Brey, University of Notre Dame men's basketball coach

"It was an absolute pleasure getting to know Steve and Lorri during Cody's recruitment and time at Indiana. I could instantly see their bond and the commitment they had in bringing out the best in one another. It is an honor to have them as part of the Indiana basketball family. Steve and Lorri provide a blueprint on how to keep family and faith first in the unbelievably competitive world of college and professional sports. Their life experiences can and will serve as an inspiration to others."

Tom Crean, Indiana University men's basketball coach

CONTENTS

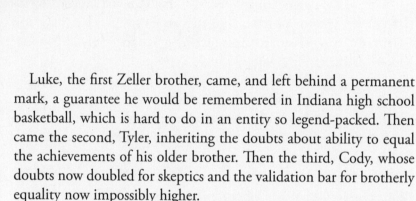

FOREWORD
by Bob Hammel

Luke, the first Zeller brother, came, and left behind a permanent mark, a guarantee he would be remembered in Indiana high school basketball, which is hard to do in an entity so legend-packed. Then came the second, Tyler, inheriting the doubts about ability to equal the achievements of his older brother. Then the third, Cody, whose doubts now doubled for skeptics and the validation bar for brotherly equality now impossibly higher.

And then their era was over—the Zeller era—and Indiana, where basketball is borderline-religious, had two other new heroes: parents Steve and Lorri Zeller, whose first names weren't even generally known but their last was as respected as it was renowned throughout Hoosierland. Steve and Lorri were the subjects, the "they" in two questions that were asked in wowed wonder in just about every Indiana assemblage imaginable:

1) How did they do it—raise kids like that?
2) Why didn't they have more?

Granted, No. 2 is a little nosy, but where production or reproduction of basketball prodigies is involved, curiosity and genuine puzzlement have no prudency bounds in Indiana.

And even that question is answered within these pages, with more enthusiasm on one side of the production team than the other.

But the first is the heart of the book, its *raison d'être*—how *did* they raise kids like that? Dad and Mom address that question almost from beginning to end, and it qualifies as must reading for young parents. It shows them and all the rest of us that The Zeller Boys didn't turn out as they did by happenstance or luck.

Dad and Mom can and do tell parts of the story that no one else could know. But Dad and Mom Zeller, simply because of modesty constraints stemming from who and what they are, can't be as sweeping and merited in describing the achievements of their three sons in a sport that is Indiana's lifeblood.

That's where I come in: an observer, an admirer, a scribe, a historian of seventy years of Indiana basketball. I can say what Steve and Lorri can't: There has never been anything like their sons in Hoosier basketball accomplishments.

I grew up disciplined in journalism to never say never. I repeat, about the Zellers: *never, anything* like them.

Since 1939, "Mr. Basketball" has been the highest honor available to an Indiana high school senior player. The Zellers were the first family to have three.

Each of the Zeller kids played on at least one State championship team. Together, they own six State championship rings.

Each of the Zeller boys was a near straight-A student, tops in his high school class.

Never. Never. Never.

Each went on to different schools to play in the top level of college basketball.

Each made it to the NBA.

Each isn't at all bashful about carrying a Bible around. Reading it occasionally. Citing it.

And each is a happy, fun-loving, prank-playing, quick-quipping kid.

How *did* Steve and Lorri do it?

Why *didn't* they have more?

Turn the pages.

by Bob Hammel,
Indiana Journalism Hall of Fame,
Indiana Basketball Hall of Fame

INTRODUCTION
by Steve & Lorri Zeller

We love country music. If you visited our southern Indiana home today, country music would most likely be playing in the background. If you traveled with us to watch any of our sons—Luke, Tyler, or Cody—play basketball, it would most likely be playing on the radio.

Country music, in its purity, has a way of taking us back, whether it's to our roots in Iowa or our memories in Indiana. There is something refreshing about its message and melodies, its emphasis on faith and simplicity, its storytelling and transparency. Though our tendency is to crowd our minds with doubt and worry, a good country song can make you slow down, breathe again, and see this life for what it really is.

We hope this book has the elements of a good, country song.

Faith. Simplicity. Storytelling. Transparency.

Along with referencing plenty of country songs throughout the book, each chapter also contains commentary from our boys. We wanted to include their input for a couple of reasons. First, we thought it might make for a more entertaining read. Second, we believe some of the most valuable parenting lessons you can learn in this life can come from your children. Luke's comments throughout the manuscript are often relatively deep, Tyler's are usually brief, and Cody's are mostly playful and sarcastic.

So, whether you are a basketball enthusiast, or a mother, father, daughter, or son, we hope our story helps you enjoy the ride God is taking you on within the story of your family and your life. We don't claim to have the answers to parenting; we only claim to have learned a lot.

And we are still learning.

by Steve and Lorri Zeller

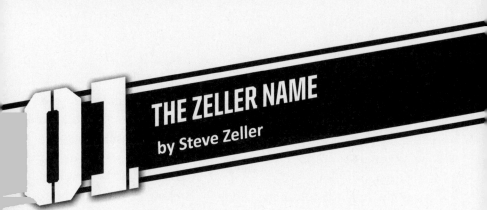

01.

THE ZELLER NAME

by Steve Zeller

We always slept in our underwear because the farmhouse was so hot.

I slept on the top bunk, which only made it warmer, in a room with three of my five brothers. That sounds like a lot, but I had six sisters, too.

I grew up on a forty-eight-acre farm in Springville, Iowa, and I was the youngest of twelve children. There were five bedrooms in our house (counting one that really was an attic). That was one for my parents and four for us children. There was only one bathroom. If there's one thing we were good at, it was sharing.

We didn't have a whole lot, but we had each other. Every autumn before we went back to school, my parents gave each of us a pair of shoes to wear for the year—to go to school in, to play sports in, to farm in, everything. By the second semester, my shoes would be all dark and gray, not from the dirt on the farm or football field, but because they'd be so worn down and falling apart that I had to wrap them in duct tape to hold them together, layer upon layer, bandaged like a wound.

The tags on my shirts never said "Eddie Bauer" or "Ralph Lauren"; they would say the names of my brothers, all crossed out in permanent marker.

~~Dean~~

~~Bob~~

~~Mark~~

~~Ted~~

~~Joel~~
Steve

Whenever one of us had a birthday, we were allowed to pick a meal for my mom, Fern Zeller, to cook. She would bake a cake, too. The first birthday present I ever received—that wasn't food—was a flannel shirt from my future wife, Lorri, when we started dating in high school.

Some might consider my childhood lacking in material things. I never thought about it. It was all I knew, and life was good enough just living on the farm with my family.

Some of the kids at school had a little more—they were the "city kids." Their parents worked in factories, from sunrise to sundown; they had nicer things and their shoes weren't covered in duct tape. But the thing about the city kids is they didn't get to see their parents as much.

We were farmers, and we farmed *together*, as family. We liked it that way. We actually believed we had *more* than the city kids because of all the time we were able to spend with our parents, because of all the time we were able to spend with each other. Life was good.

One summer, however, we thought we were going to lose my dad—Joseph Zeller, the rock of our family.

It was July 1972, and I was nine years old. It had been a difficult year. Three of my close relatives, including two uncles, had passed away due to brain aneurysms—a weak vessel in the brain that if it blew out, like a bubble on a tire, would cause a hemorrhage, which is how President Franklin Roosevelt died. Dad figured he should go to the hospital and get his head checked out to see if it ran in the family. It did. Doctors told him that he, too, had an aneurysm.

With Dad being a farmer and Mom working at home raising twelve children, we didn't have a ton of extra money floating around to pay for a major surgery. But it wasn't optional—that's how serious and pressing his aneurysm was. Doctors told him if he didn't get it taken care of, he would inevitably die from it. All of our minds ran wild. What would we do without Dad? How could our family even survive?

A couple of weeks after his diagnosis, Mom and Dad left the farm and drove up to Rochester, Minnesota, for surgery at the Mayo Clinic, leaving the older kids in charge. This was a big deal—Dad never left the farm, not to mention the entire state of Iowa.

The night before Dad's surgery, I remember stripping down to my underwear and climbing into my bed on the top bunk as I always did. I couldn't fall asleep, however; all I could think about was Dad, and all the people in our family who kept "leaving." My first experiences with death had hit me like a hurricane. I stared at the ceiling wide-eyed for an hour or two, unable to turn off my brain. What did it all mean? What was death? What if Dad never returned?

I became frantic and upset. My brothers were sound asleep, so there was no one to talk to. One of my brothers was snoring.

I'm not sure what came over me, but I felt like I needed to get down on the floor. I climbed out of my bed and stood in the middle of the room. I slowly shrank to the floor until I was on both of my knees.

I'm not even sure if I truly knew what praying was, but that was what I was about to do. In a way, it was all I *could* do. We went to Mass every Sunday as a family, and I had recited the "Hail Mary" and the "Our Father," and the "Glory Be" plenty of times, but never had I prayed—*really prayed*—on my own before. *Never* had I prayed in my own words.

"God," I said, "please be with Dad."

Not knowing what else to say, I made the sign of the cross, stood up, got back in my bed, and went to sleep.

It was the first time I ever depended on God.

Around the time Dad had his surgery, I was collecting box tops from cereal boxes to buy a poster of a lion. I was going to hang it on the wall next to my bunk bed. I'm sure the poster only cost a dollar or so, and I told my brother Mark how excited I was to buy the poster.

"Well," Mark told me, "if Dad never comes back, we won't be able to afford *food,* including cereal."

Dad's surgery terrified us.

He had the procedure, and we heard it went well, but he and Mom stayed in Minnesota for several weeks while Dad recovered. "Bizarre" is the only word that describes that time in our house. Twelve children left to fend for themselves. We could maintain the farm and do our chores, but without our parents, we were a rudderless ship. We had no direction, no hope, without the foundation of our family—our parents. We were lost.

When it finally came time for Mom and Dad to leave Minnesota and return home, they had their own difficulties. Mom had to drive Dad back to Iowa while he lay on a thick, six-inch piece of Styrofoam on the floor of our family vehicle. She got him successfully back to Iowa, but the father we were so excited and relieved to see wasn't the one we expected. We had never seen him so weak before. We were scared, shaken.

Dad was your typical "man's man," a strong, hard-working father who spent grueling sixteen-hour days on the farm, so it was truly uncomfortable to see him helpless. The father we knew could fix anything he touched with his giant, rough, and calloused hands that had worked through the Great Depression and World War II. Now, he couldn't fix his own self.

Farming was Dad's *chosen* work, his passion. He was at his best at home raising and caring for the animals. He took great pride in planting and harvesting his crops. It was in his blood.

Growing up on the farm, the land and animals always came first. It sometimes seemed like they came before us, but now I understand that they came first *for* us. We never left the dinner table hungry, thanks to Dad.

Overall, the best word that described him was "strength." Dad was an American World War II veteran with a rich German background, and since he was blind in one eye, he was one of the last local men drafted for the war. Dad could be an intimidating person, too. When he put his foot down, nobody wanted to be under it. If I ever ran in the house, he would punish me by making me run in place while he thwacked my bottom over and over with a Funk's G seed corn yardstick. He had his rules, and he never wavered from them.

Dad wasn't one to show affection, either. When I was younger, he would sometimes be reclining in his chair after a long day's work, and I'd hop on his lap and tell him, "Good night." I'd kiss him on the cheek, and he would make a funny expression or rub his whiskery chin on my face and give me a beard burn. I would laugh and squirm. This was the way he showed he loved me, though I never remember him actually saying the words, "I love you."

Mom also didn't show much affection, probably because she never had much affection shown to her. She was constantly moving—cooking, cleaning, and raising all twelve of her children—hardly ever having enough time to really *enjoy* whatever phase of life she was in. She always amazed me with her mastery of the art of multitasking. Sometimes, she would be toasting bread in the toaster while also toasting bread in the oven so she could serve us our food at the same time. She squeezed six cents out of every nickel. Whenever she fried bacon, she would use the bacon grease to fry the eggs. She was a consummate farmer's wife—taking care of her children while her husband worked a hundred hours a week in the fields. She was *always* busy, never more so than during this period where she was also taking care of Dad, hoping she wouldn't lose him.

After several weeks, Dad finally started to act like himself again. He returned to work, and our family life again felt normal. He had recovered from a complicated surgery, and we resumed our simple ways. �֍

Life on the farm went back to normal again.

We children would wake up each morning at five o'clock, and we would all milk the cows, and feed the hogs, chicken, and sheep before school. Then we would eat breakfast together in the kitchen. That's the way Mom and Dad raised us: to put the animals' stomachs before our own.

CODY: One of my favorite stories about Grandpa came from this period when he had his surgery. Because he was so limited in what he could do, he had to put his family on food stamps. When he got his feet back under him, he went to the offices and told them he wanted to set up a payment plan so that he could pay back the food stamps. They told him he didn't have to, but he insisted on paying them back. I bet he's one of the few people to ever do that. The world needs more people like him.

We would board the bus at seven thirty in the morning for a fifty-minute bus ride to school, longer than most because we lived deeper in the country than almost anyone else. We would go to school, get out at three o'clock in the afternoon, and be home by four. That gave us thirty minutes to play before our chores started again.

Mom would start peeling potatoes late in the afternoon for a six thirty, fourteen-person supper. We would complete our chores, milk the cows and feed the animals again, eat supper together, finish our homework, then be in bed by nine. Sometimes, if we completed our chores in good time, Dad would join us for a game of baseball after supper. Those times would be the highlight of our day.

The next day, we'd start the routine all over again. On the weekend, with no school, we would work with Mom in the garden.

Mom ran our home, raising all twelve children. It was a traditional home with a non-traditional amount of kids, so, typical Catholics.

There was a simplicity to the way we lived, and this simplicity seemed to produce joy. We lived off the land. We relied on the sun. We relied on the rain. We relied on a good harvest to have a good year. From the very get-go, I was taught to appreciate what God gave us, even something like an afternoon shower, its storm clouds sweeping across the flat, golden Iowa fields. �֎

Mom and Dad taught us to appreciate what God had given us, and they also taught us to work hard.

This was our way of life on the farm. Depending on the weather, on God. Depending on one another. Simplicity.

LUKE: Reading about Dad's childhood helps explain a lot as to why he raised us the way he did. Grandma and Grandpa were amazing people, and I can see why Dad implemented a lot of the same principles with us.

Mom and Dad had a simple way of parenting, too.

If one of us got in trouble throughout the day, the kid in trouble would have to confess his or her transgressions to Dad in front of the entire family at the dinner table. Dad was so intimidating, and there were so many of us, it was a humiliating experience that we all dreaded.

Once, I threw a baseball through the dining room window earlier in the day, and I remember being so ashamed as Dad glared at me from across the dinner table that evening. He knew exactly what I had done—a breeze was even blowing into our house through the shattered window—but I was *still* afraid to admit it to him. It truly hurt to let him down, internally due to my shame and externally due to my post-dinner spanking in the backyard.

The way we conducted ourselves was always one of my parents' primary concerns—not only within our household but also away from our household.

Dad, for example, always talked to us about "the Zeller name." He would talk about it like it was a fortress to defend or a castle to build, like everything we did or didn't do in life would either add to its elevation or contribute to its decline. He raised us to take pride in our last name. Dad always talked about the long history of people who helped build up the Zeller name. How irreparably shameful would it be if someone dishonored it? Whenever I hear country artist Dierks Bentley's song "My Last Name," I am reminded of my upbringing.

Ultimately, all talk of the Zeller name pointed us toward something bigger than ourselves. Having to admit our sins in front of the entire family at dinner was one thing (and believe me, the spanking hurt), but embarrassing the entire family name was another thing. Making the right decision seemed to be much easier once I realized making a wrong decision would hurt the very people who loved me and shared my name.

Just as it was important not to shame the Zeller name, Dad said it was also important to continue building it. There might have been rules, but obedience also presented an opportunity. Building the Zeller name, he explained, was not accomplished by your performance on the football field in high school or being successful in your career after college, but rather by being a good human being. If you borrowed a lawn mower from a neighbor, for instance, it needed to be returned with a full tank of gas, checked for oil, and cleaned thoroughly. It was your responsibility to give it back to the owner in better condition than it was when you borrowed it.

Mom and Dad were among the most generous people I've ever known. Despite having twelve children, despite being what some might consider "poor," they were always doing favors for others, expecting nothing in return. They truly lived by the Golden Rule and therefore found no need to establish an exchange system. They didn't get hung up on who had given more or less. They went through life walking alongside others. They didn't have business partners, they had friends. There is freedom in genuine relationships because you aren't caught up in the bondage of "fairness."

They taught us that walking alongside each other through life, shoulder to shoulder, breaks down the complicated exchange systems that bind us. This is one of the most beautiful things about relationships—they make life more enjoyable while also making you a better person, much like our relationship with God.

When Dad talked about the Zeller name, it really made me feel like I was part of something bigger than myself—that my actions, whether good or bad, would affect more than just me, that I was either adding a brick to the Zeller fortress or removing one. This became our definition of success: upholding the Zeller name.

Without a doubt, these "old school" principles—work before play, putting others before yourself, honoring the Zeller name—influenced the way my wife, Lorri, and I raised our sons: Luke, Tyler, and Cody. That is why this is the first chapter of the book—because nothing influenced me more as a parent than the way my parents raised me. Perhaps the simple, hard-working, humble lifestyle of a Midwestern Catholic family in Iowa can be a clarifying breath of fresh air in a complicated, chaotic society.

For my parents, upholding the Zeller name meant unleashing children into the world who were better than themselves. Of course, they shaped and molded us through discipline and concepts like "the Zeller name," but they also did this through loving us. They came alongside us. They supported us. They wanted us to know that no one loved us more than they did—that, even if they were disciplining us, it was because they loved us.

Dad might not have been one to say "I love you," but I always knew he did. And I think that's why I will always remember the Christmas Eve of 1968—it was one of the few times that he expressed his love for me in a very personal way. Though I was only six years old, I remember it like it was yesterday.

We loved Christmas Eve because it was our one day out of the entire year to unwrap our presents. We would attend Christmas Eve Mass as a family and return home to find a box of presents on our front porch. All of the younger kids would exclaim, "Santa came!" but the older kids knew that not Joseph and Mary but my siblings Chuck and Mary had snuck off and placed our presents on the porch. Then, we would take the presents inside and open them in our living room. There was no feeling like it. Strangely, I don't even remember what gift I received that '68 Christmas Eve.

After unwrapping presents, we would pile our gifts in the corners of the living room, clean up the debris left over from twelve rowdy children, and play cards together on the floor.

Dad also had a tradition every Christmas Eve. He would walk through the living room and gather the wrapping paper. He would put it in a big, black trash bag, and take it outside. On this particular Christmas Eve, I decided to go outside with Dad.

I put on my coat and followed him out the door. It was below freezing outside but also a rare Iowa night where the cold, winter wind wasn't sweeping across the flatlands and whistling outside the walls of our house like an oncoming train.

Everything was calm. The moon was out. And it was just my dad and me. We weren't talking. We were just together.

We went back behind the garage to burn the wrapping paper. I watched him, as if memorizing his every move, as he meticulously placed each piece of torn-up wrapping paper in a large fifty-gallon drum we used as a trash barrel.

We children knew that lighting a fire was a ritual for Dad. He couldn't just light a piece of paper and dump the rest on top. It had to be *perfect* before he struck his match. He would place each piece of paper on top of the other. Not too fast. Not too slow. His way, the only way.

Dad took out a match and held it in his calloused hand. I knew he had only one match, because he always had only one match. Having ventured through the Great Depression, he was conservative with everything. That included matches. Dad scraped the match across his thumb. Really, his thumb. And I saw a little flame flicker in his fingertips, then fall into the trash barrel.

The paper caught fire.

I smiled.

The flames grew and grew, producing warmth on a cold Christmas Eve and some light on our dark farm. I was mesmerized as I watched the flames dance back and forth, back and forth, as if the fire was breathing.

A tiny piece of paper floated out of the barrel, taking flight, and I watched the orange glow climb toward one of the three oak trees behind our garage. It gently landed on a branch and dissolved.

I was amazed by the beauty, the stillness, of it all.

Dad and I stood there, watching the paper take flight from the barrel, then disappear.

He didn't say anything.

Neither did I.

Somewhere in that moment, Dad reached down and grabbed my hand. I looked down at our hands, shocked because he had never done anything like this before, then up at Dad. He was looking out into our yard, naturally stone-faced and emotionless—unfazed.

I smiled. The best Christmas gift I ever received.

Dad's calloused hands felt very soft that night.

02 DUST DATE
by Lorri Zeller

My background was very much like Steve's. I also came from a farming family, and my dad, Marv Eberhard, could also be intimidating and somewhat terrifying—especially toward someone who was trying to date me, like Steve.

My family had a little more money because my parents had three children, not twelve, but we were humble farmers nonetheless, living off the land and depending on God for the rain. I had two brothers: Dale, who was twelve years older than me, and Al, nine years older than me. Dale left for college when I was in kindergarten, so I always felt we were in such different stages of life that it was tough to develop a close relationship. Still, we were family.

Al was around the house a little bit more, and he was the pride of Springville, Iowa. He played college basketball for the University of Missouri and was drafted by the Detroit Pistons in the first round of the 1974 NBA Draft. Whenever Detroit played Chicago or Milwaukee—the two closest cities to Springville—our town would get a charter bus and travel through the Iowa farmland up to Chicago or Milwaukee in support of Al.

Al was drafted before ESPN's grand spectacle of Draft Day and before anyone even knew what a "green room" was. He was actually out back planting corn when the owner of the Detroit Pistons called. Al eventually came inside, and my mom, Hazel Eberhard, said to him, "Someone who sounded important called; you may want to give him a call back." Al called him back and found out he had been drafted.

Once he signed his contract, Al said to Dad, "I don't have any use for this money that they are paying me."

"Well," Dad said, "want to build a machine shed?"

So the two of them took the money and bought supplies for a machine shed.

Classic farmers. ❀

It was through Al, actually, that our family connected with the Zellers. Al and Steve happened to wear the same shoe size, so, even before Steve and I started dating, Steve would come over and Al would let him pick out a pair of sneakers before basketball season. Size thirteen. Canvas-white, Converse All-Star Chuck Taylor low-tops.

Steve's parents would get him one pair of shoes per year, but they would usually be pretty torn up by the time basketball season rolled around. Al had plenty of shoes from playing in the NBA. In our little farming town, everyone seemed to be connected, and everyone seemed to have each other's backs.

꧁꧂

Steve and I were high school sweethearts.

Our first date was the summer before his junior year and my senior year. He came to pick me up at my family's farmhouse, which was down a long gravel road a quarter-

---

CODY: Some of our favorite childhood memories come from our visits to Grandpa's farm in Iowa. We always played on his farm equipment and made up our own games. No surprise, it always seemed to get pretty competitive amongst us brothers, even in the littlest games.

One day, Grandpa was out farming, and he brought back a full load of corn. Tyler and I were on top of the wagon, watching the corn below our feet flow into the auger, which led to the grain bin for storage. I'm not sure where Luke was. As the corn flowed out the bottom, it created a funnel/tornado effect/suction at the top. Tyler and I came up with a game of putting our feet in the funnel, as it sucked our legs into the corn. We decided that whoever was sucked deepest into the corn would win our game.

TYLER: We usually pulled our legs out of the corn once our calves were sucked in, but then Cody got greedy. Trying to break my record, he went a little too far, was sucked in past his knees, and couldn't pull himself out. I couldn't pull him out, either.

CODY: I kept getting sucked in more and more, as if it was quicksand, all the way to my chest. I yelled for help.

TYLER: No, you "cried" for help.

CODY: Whatever. Luckily, Dad and Uncle Al (Mom's brother) were watching the wagon unload down below, and they finally got the message to shut the door to the auger. The corn flow stopped, and they climbed into the wagon to pull me out.

TYLER: I guess that's what Cody gets for thinking he could beat me in something.

mile off the highway.

He knocked on the front door, and I let him in. When he walked inside, my mother was in the kitchen, and my father was in his recliner. Mom, Steve, and I were all talking, while Dad remained relatively quiet, staring at the wall in front of him and occasionally sipping on his daily beer.

What made my dad most intimidating was his size. Dad had hands like the Hulk and wore a size fourteen ring. His fingers are probably three times the size of mine.

Dad had just finished drinking his beer, and he sat the can on the arm of his recliner. He started pretending to get mad about something (I think he was trying to intimidate Steve), complaining to Mom about this thing he was "mad" about.

Dad flicked the can with one of his massive fingers, making a loud *ping* sound, and it flew across our living room and landed right next to Steve's feet. It looked like Dad had taken his fist and crushed one side of the can through the other.

Steve looked down at it . . . gulped . . . then looked over at Dad. Their eyes met from across the room.

"What time would you like your daughter home?" Steve asked.

Steve picked me up in the only car his family had—a big, old, International Travelall that could haul around his eleven brothers and sisters. The floorboards and door frames inside were so rusted out, it left orange on your skin if you touched it.

"There is a movie starting at seven o'clock," Steve told me when I got in the car. "It's *Rocky II*. Wanna see it?"

"Yes, that sounds great," I told him.

"How do you get there?" he asked me.

Turns out, Steve had hardly been off the farm and into the city. The farm was all he knew. Nor did he bother to ask for directions from his parents, apparently.

The movie was at Stage 4 Theater in Cedar Rapids, about an hour's drive. My mother and I would go to the city and shop every once in a while on the weekends. I knew how to get there, so we made our way down the gravel road.

Within the first minute or two of our date, all the time I spent getting ready was ruined by the Travelall. The holes in the Travelall's wheel wells pushed so much dust from our driveway into the vehicle that I couldn't even see Steve, who was sitting right next to me.

I coughed, we both laughed, and the dust slowly dissipated as we pulled onto the highway—the very beginning of the lifelong road we would travel together.

That night, he met Dad's wishes and had me home by ten thirty.

⸎

Steve and I had a friendship before we started dating.

I always knew the Zellers as the most athletic family in town. His five older brothers played basketball and football, and my family was engrossed in the sports world themselves—all of us played basketball. When Steve first came to pick out a pair of shoes at our house, I said hello, but never imagined he'd be my husband. ⚫

Turns out Steve and I had many of the same friends the next two years, even though I was a year ahead of him in school. Our high school had a study hall for honor roll students, and Steve and I were

CODY: Dad never talks about it, but he had thirty rebounds in a high school basketball game when he and Mom were dating—which broke Al's previous school record. Grandma told me the next few times Dad went over to see Mom, Grandma wouldn't even talk to Dad because she was upset that he broke Al's record.

in there together with about six other people. We didn't really study all that much, but sometimes Steve would help me with algebra or calculus. ❁

My junior year, I asked Steve to my prom. He originally turned down my invitation because he said he didn't have anything to wear. But he borrowed his brother's suit jacket and combined it with some navy blue pants. He had a rust-colored tie, and I had a red boutonniere for him. It didn't match, but I had the date that I wanted.

CODY: Yeah, Mom, I'm sure you really "struggled" with math. Sure you weren't just faking it so you could ask Dad for help?

When Steve picked me up for prom, we talked to Mom inside, but Dad was out disking the field. Mom said we should go out to the field and show Dad how nice we looked. We did.

Dad was on the other side of the field when we approached him. He saw us and walked across the field and up to the fence, where we stood. He said we looked nice. He was never the emotional type, like Steve's dad. He just smiled and told us to have fun.

My father is also the king of one-liners. As we left the fence line and started walking back toward the vehicle, we heard him yell, "Hey!"

We turned around.

"Just don't do anything you'll regret nine months from now." ❁

TYLER: Oh. My.

ᴧᴧᴧᴧᴧ

Steve and I started dating the summer after prom, which began with our little "dust date" to the city. Dad always called Steve "Zeller Boy." I think Dad always found it fun (in a very twisted way) to try to intimidate Steve.

We didn't go on very many dates throughout high school because neither of us had much money, so we mostly hung out and spent time together. Many evenings, Steve would come over, and we would watch Johnny Carson on our living room couch. One night, we started kissing, and Steve removed his glasses. ❁

⇐ ✸

LUKE: Seriously?

TYLER: Uhhhhhhhh...

CODY: Why are you writing about this?

We could always tell if Dad was making his way around the house because we could hear the echo of his crackly knees. That night, however, we didn't hear Dad walk through the living room as Steve and I kissed on the couch. The first thing we noticed was the bathroom light turn on, which meant Dad had walked through the living room (while we were kissing) and into the bathroom. Steve sat up in a nervous sweat, quickly putting his glasses back on. We heard the toilet flush, Dad flipped off the bathroom light, and he walked through the living room.

"Probably easier to watch television with your glasses on, Zeller Boy," Dad said, walking back into his bedroom.

Busted.

Always after a date, when Steve brought me home, Mom would start flipping our porch lights off and on, as if to say, "Hurry up, we don't know what you are doing in there."

That's just how old-fashioned my family was.

Steve and I dated for a couple years before breaking up when he went to college at Iowa State. I went to Central College in Pella, Iowa, my freshman year before transferring my sophomore year to Coe College, which was much closer to home.

We both dated different people his freshman semester, but it wasn't the same. Steve dated a girl who was a hippie-type with a belief-system revolving around the cosmos and surrendering control to the ways of the universe. That relationship didn't last very long. He learned that one of the essentials to finding the right spouse was having a worldview based on the same foundations.

The guy I dated was a slightly more serious relationship. He came from a wealthy family that attended a Lutheran church. I struggled with the relationship because it wasn't the same as dating Steve, but I remember my mom telling me, "Lorri, you can love a rich Lutheran just as well as you can love a poor Catholic." She really liked my Lutheran boyfriend.

However, I was learning a thing or two about relationships, too.

I learned that one of the essentials to finding the right spouse was being able to have fun together, enjoy hanging out together, and be able to talk with one another endlessly. Today, too much emphasis is placed on the physical side of relationships, when, in all reality, this is one of the least important things. If your worldviews align, if you have fun together, and if you are attracted to one another, your relationship will be much more long-lasting than something based on emotions and surface-level thinking.

Our semester apart, Steve used the entire fall and winter to make me a cassette tape of songs. There was no such thing as burning a CD or making an iTunes playlist back then, so the only way to put a compilation of songs together was to listen to the radio at the right time, catch a song, and record it onto a cassette tape. Steve would sit in the dorm next to his radio and wait for a particular song to play, or he would make a phone call to the radio station and request a song he needed to record. He would narrate between each song and explain its sentimental value in the context of his relationship with me. ❁

When he returned home for Christmas break, he gave me the cassette. That was really something. I can't imagine how long it took him to do that. I don't remember

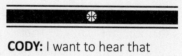

CODY: I want to hear that cassette!!!

many of the songs on there, but one of them was "Lady" by Kenny Rogers.

However, there was one problem: I was still dating the rich Lutheran boy my mother wanted me to marry. One day over Christmas break, Steve came over to check on me to see how I was feeling after I had gotten my tonsils removed earlier that morning. While Steve was over, my boyfriend at the time also called our house phone to see if I had made it back from the hospital. To this day, Steve swears I talked to him on the phone for an hour and a half. I can't imagine it could have been more than fifteen minutes. Whatever the case, Steve eventually stormed out of the house and peeled out of our gravel driveway in his Chevy Nova, his college car. (The next time Dad saw Steve, he said, "Hey, Zeller Boy, you might want to put some of that gravel back on the driveway that you shot off onto the lawn the other day when you left.")

Of course, I eventually got back together with Steve. We started dating again on Valentine's Day, just a couple of months later, and we never looked back.

Also, we played "Lady" by Kenny Rogers on our wedding day.

᙭᙭᙭

Over the next three and a half years we dated from a distance, writing letters to one another every day, calling every Sunday night, seeing one another on holidays, and taking the Greyhound bus to meet up with each other once a month if Steve had a break from his pre-vet studies and I wasn't in basketball season.

Every day, my roommate and I would get our mail from the campus post office before lunch and read letters from our boyfriends while we were eating. Sometimes the letters would get lost in the mail, so I would have two or three to read in one day. Steve wrote me every day. And I wrote him every day. Steve also wrote poems. ✿

Those are stored some place safe where our boys will never find them.

Steve and I got "promised" his junior year, which was, in a nutshell, making the commitment we wanted to spend our lives togeth-er—but without being engaged. It was the thing to do back then. Cody jokes that the diamond on my promise ring is smaller than the tip of a sharpened pencil. But it was perfect to me.

LUKE: Wow.

TYLER: Wow.

CODY: Wow.

I graduated from college, and I knew Steve was making payments on an engagement ring during his senior year because I helped him pick the ring out at a local family jewelry business. Back then, getting promised felt like a much bigger deal than getting engaged. Steve had a job laying sod to pay for the ring, and whatever he made basically went straight to the jewelry store. He finally made his last payment on the ring by spring break in March.

One day over spring break, Steve came over to my parents' house and walked through the door carrying an end table for some reason.

"Did you stop at the jewelry store and pick up the ring?" I asked him.

"No, they didn't have it ready," he told me.

I sighed.

"But I went to my sister's house, and she had this table she doesn't want anymore," he told me. (We were starting to gather furniture for our future home.)

"Okay?" I said, finding his transition from the ring to a table strange.

Well," he said, "aren't you going to open the drawers?"

I opened the drawer and saw the ring inside.

It wasn't the most romantic thing, but we knew we were getting engaged anyway. I shrieked and put the ring on my finger, soon to find out that it hadn't been sized. It got stuck on my finger, and I had to go back to the jeweler, get it cut off, and have them craft a brand new ring. We were engaged, nonetheless.

In June 1985, Steve graduated, found a job in the meat-processing industry, married me, and we went on our honeymoon—all in a two-week span.

On our wedding day, Dad approached Steve after the ceremony and thumped him in the chest in a congratulatory way. Dad could do the simplest things and hurt people because he was so strong. Steve says it knocked the wind out of him.

"You better treat her right," Dad ordered.

"Of course," Steve coughed, holding his chest.

Other than the cassette tape, Steve wasn't the most romantic guy in the world, but he respected me, and he treated me like his queen. I've always felt dearly loved by Steve on a deep level, both during our dating relationship and through our marriage. Our boys know the right way to treat and pursue a woman, not because of what we've told them, but because of the way Steve treats me and the way they watched Steve respect me as they grew up. If you want your children to treat their significant other the right way, it's important for you to model it in your own relationship.

Our oldest boy, Luke, married his wife, Hope, in 2010, and Tyler married his wife, Caitlyn, in the summer of 2014. They took purity, respect, and the decision to get married seriously. As we look at our children today, it's those kind of things that make us most proud, not the fact they made it to the NBA. As much as we enjoy traveling the country and watching their games, it's their character that makes us smile most.

The purpose behind sharing our dating story and even talking about our relationship is because the relationship between two parents is one of the foundations of parenting. When a marriage thrives, it makes parenting that much easier because the husband and wife are operating as one cohesive unit. It is much easier to tackle parenting as a team, rather than as individuals.

This concept can just as easily be applied to those who have divorced. Just because a marriage may have fallen apart does not mean that the two parents should not still try to operate as a team in how they raise the child they brought into this world together. It may be more difficult because of the strife or the baggage, but it is best for the sake of their children if two divorced parents can do their best to operate as a team.

I once heard parenting in the context of marriage compared to flying on an airplane. When the flight attendant goes through the safety instructions before takeoff, he or she encourages passengers—in the case of an emergency where oxygen masks might be needed—to first put the mask on yourself before you put it on your children. The purpose of doing so, of course, is because the adult will be able to handle the situation with more caution, care, and control if he or she is safe. The children, ultimately, have a better chance of being safe if the parent first has things under control.

This couldn't be truer in marriage. There are too many parents first putting oxygen masks on their children, and, consequently, their marriage is running out of air. Raising children, strangely, can sometimes destroy a marriage if you neglect your relationship with your spouse.

Honestly, focusing on our marriage did indeed become more difficult once Steve and I started having kids. When we had our first son, Luke, several of our friends told us it was important to try to carve out time once a month for a date. Sometimes we did a good job and went on a date that month. Other times we struggled and maybe it was only once every couple of months. But our friends were definitely right. Dates are more important when you're married than when you are dating.

As we had Tyler three years after Luke and Cody three years after Tyler, Steve and I learned how important it was to continually bring our relationship to the forefront, not only for the sake of our own health, but also for the sake of our children.

Our goal was always to do our best to work it out and never go to bed angry at one another as Ephesians 4:26 addresses: "'In your anger do not sin': Do not let the sun go down while you are still angry." We took this principle very seriously.

It is within the confines of two parents working together as a team that children are molded and shaped most effectively. They will respect a team more than an individual. The stronger the team, the stronger the parenting.

03

BA DA BA BA BA

by Steve Zeller

Childbirth seems to be a pretty fitting beginning to something as wild as parenthood. It's as if, from the very start, God is saying, "Just wanted to paint a realistic picture for you of what is to come."

And yet, even in something as both painful and phenomenal as childbirth, there is no greater feeling than holding your child for the first time—it's understandable why George Strait would have a song called "I Saw God Today" about the birth of his child. And, similarly, there is nothing more meaningful and fulfilling in this world than pouring your own life into your children's lives, despite how difficult it is.

I know I have no grounds to make a claim regarding the pain involved in childbirth, since I'm a man and all, but then again, based on what I've seen, maybe I do. All I know is this: It takes a remarkable woman to birth three seven-footers.

<hr/>

We were honestly surprised our children ended up being so tall. We've been told that tallness is often received from the mother's side, and, though I'm not sure if this is a fact or not, it is certainly true in our case. I am six foot four—the tallest of all twelve of my brothers and sisters—and Lorri is six feet tall. Tallness didn't really run in my family, but it did in Lorri's. Her brother Al, who played in the NBA, was six foot six. What is even more bizarre than our children's height, however, is that each of their birth stories seem to fit their personalities perfectly. I will explain this in the coming pages.

We were still living in Iowa when Lorri was pregnant with Luke, as I was working nights at Oscar Mayer in the meat products division. Typically, Lorri went to the doctor's office alone while I slept. I didn't like it to be that way; it's just the way it had to be. Eventually, however, my boss moved my shift to the daytime, which allowed me to go with Lorri to one of her appointments, one month before her due date.

I was pretty excited to go with her—to hear the doctor talk about *our* child, to see our little baby on the monitor, to experience it all *with* Lorri. The fact that I was about to become a father was beginning to become strangely real to me. This appointment, I figured, would make it *very* real.

The day of her appointment, I got off work at Oscar Mayer and drove straight to Farm Credit Services, where Lorri was working. I had worked through my lunch break that day in order to leave early, so, needless to say, by the time I picked up Lorri, I was absolutely starved. I was a young buck, only twenty-four years old, and I think I was still eating at the same pace I was in high school.

It was a forty-minute drive or so to the Mary Greeley Hospital in Ames, and, since we got to the appointment a little early, we decided to go into McDonald's and grab a bite to eat. I think I ordered a Big Mac. Lorri didn't order anything because she didn't feel very well. We sat in a booth, waiting for the cashier to call our order.

It was nice to finally sit, relax, and slow down amidst the havoc of the day—the jobs, the appointments, the to-and-fro of the work-week. Even if "slowing down" meant just sitting inside a random McDonald's in Ames for a few minutes, it was refreshing. We weren't even parents yet, but still it felt like there was never enough time in any given day.

The cashier called our order, and I walked over to the counter to pick up my food. I returned to our booth, sat down, and hurriedly unwrapped my Big Mac, practically dying to put something in my stomach for the first time since breakfast.

"We've got to go!" Lorri said.

I looked at my watch. We still had fifteen minutes before her appointment, and the hospital was literally two blocks away from Mc-

Donald's. I didn't understand why Lorri was in such a hurry.

"Yeah," I told her, somewhat dismissively, not even looking up at her, "after I finish my sandwich."

I took a bite.

"No, Steve," she quivered. "We've got to go."

I sensed the uneasiness in her voice, and I looked up at her. Her face was stamped with sheer terror.

"Steve," she said.

I looked down at the booth.

"Steve," she said again.

Her water had broken.

I was in a daze.

The booth, not to be grotesque, was absolutely *coated* in blood. It was on the seat. It was on the floor. Somehow, it was even on the table (perhaps it had gotten on her hands). It looked like a murder scene. ✱

"Let's go," I said, no longer hungry.

We both jumped from our seats. Well, I doubt Lorri "jumped."

"There's blood at that table," I said to a McDonald's manager as we walked out the door.

"Excuse me?" the manager said, lowering his eyebrows.

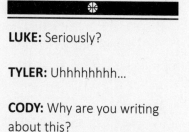

LUKE: Seriously?

TYLER: Uhhhhhhhh...

CODY: Why are you writing about this?

"There's, uh, blood at that table," I repeated.

He looked at me as if I had dropped in from Mars.

"We left blood there," I said again, pointing.

And then we bolted out of McDonald's.

I can only imagine what was running through that poor manager's mind.

We were too naïve to realize that the uncanny amount of blood was not normal. We figured that was just the way it was. We knew everything was unfolding slightly earlier than we imagined, but we were naïve in this regard as well. We had taken classes, so we knew her water would eventually break, obviously, but we didn't really know what that meant.

"I don't think it's supposed to be bloody like this," Lorri said to me, as she sat in the passenger seat of our *brand new* Monte Carlo, which I had actually just cleaned out the day before. ✳

"Oh, no, I'm sure it's completely normal," I reassured her.

Deep down, however, I wondered if this was how it was supposed to be. I looked over at the passenger's seat and noticed that her legs and feet were covered in blood. All I could do was try to keep her calm.

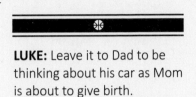

LUKE: Leave it to Dad to be thinking about his car as Mom is about to give birth.

At least we are close to the hospital, I said to myself. I tried to remain optimistic. The thing is, the situation really could have been far worse. We could have had to drive forty minutes to the hospital, but luckily, this *just so happened* to take place on the day of Lorri's appointment, and it *just so happened* to take place as we were only two blocks away from the hospital.

But my optimism struck too soon.

As I pulled out of the McDonald's parking lot, I heard the loud hum of an approaching train, followed by its obnoxious nasal-like horn.

Seriously.

We were *two* blocks from the hospital, yet the hospital was on the other side of the railroad tracks. The two blocks felt more like two hundred miles.

It seemed foolish to call an ambulance when we were only two blocks away from the hospital, but it did cross my mind. Plus, even if we *did* call an ambulance, the ambulance would be blocked by the train, too! My mind was racing, but I knew I had to remain calm for Lorri.

So, instead of getting to the hospital in less than a minute, we sat in bumper-to-bumper traffic in a standstill, watching cargo car after cargo car after cargo car scoot along into eternity.

"It's going to be okay," I told her.

Lorri nodded.

"We're almost there."

The train eventually passed, we crossed the railroad tracks, and we pulled into the hospital parking lot. But then we faced another problem.

The hospital was under construction.

In a clutter of blocked-off areas and orange cones, we had no idea where the emergency room was located. I felt like I was lugging a pregnant woman around a labyrinth.

Eventually, we found an entrance. I parked the car, opened the passenger-side door, and picked up Lorri as we journeyed toward what felt like the Promised Land.

At that moment, a nurse must have seen us, and she ran toward us as I carried Lorri across the hospital lawn.

In a moment as desperate as this, the nurse was like an angel that God had given us. She met us right where we were. She was so calm and so composed that we figured everything we were experiencing— the amount of blood, the premature circumstances, the anxiety—was completely normal.

She guided us into the hospital and into a room where a doctor quickly greeted us. "We usually don't see blood like this, but it's okay," he comforted us. "It's no big deal."

For the next three hours, Lorri was in labor.

Turns out, she had abruptio placentae, a separation of the placental lining from the uterus which causes an overabundance of bleeding. The doctor explained this to me, but I still didn't know what it meant. The events of the day were a blur. I was just happy we made it to the hospital. We felt safe.

Throughout Lorri's delivery, the doctor, nurse, and I actually got pretty bored. I know this sounds bad, but at one point, we all started playing a game and seeing who could guess the song that was being piped through the speakers of the delivery room.

"Hello!" Lorri said at one point. "Someone is having a baby here!"

"I know," I told her. Then I turned to the doctor. "I think that's U2," I said. (The superstar group had just released their *Joshua Tree* album.) ✱

Finally, at eight thirty in the evening on April 4, 1987, Lucas Joseph Zeller, named after my father Joseph Zeller, was born at seven

LUKE: Oh my gosh, Dad.

pounds, thirteen ounces, and twenty inches long. To top it all off, Lorri delivered him naturally with no pain medicines.

Now, in a perfect world, I would say it was a beautiful moment. But Luke was far from a beautiful baby. Because of Lorri's excessive bleeding, Luke had swallowed some blood in the womb. This altered his entire color, and, as I held my son and entered my initial moments of fatherhood, all I could think about was how my firstborn, jaundiced son looked more like a lizard than a human being. The doctor told us not to be concerned, however. They ran several tests, and Luke was completely healthy apart from the visual. His entire body was a purplish-pink, and he had white splotches and polka dots all over him. I couldn't stop thinking about the reptile of a thing I was holding.

Lorri studied Luke as I held him, mostly perplexed and perhaps a little bit disgusted. I handed him to her.

"All that work for *this*?" Lorri joked, holding Luke for the first time. I shrugged.

"This thing looks awful," she said, handing him back to me. ✵

We laughed. Life isn't perfection—it's far from it—but having fun and laughing along the way with those you love can make it strangely per-fect.

LUKE: I feel so loved, guys.

The blood shed in McDonald's.

The train.

The hospital renovations.

All leading up to, not a picturesque/Hollywood moment, but rather, the spawn of something that could be cousins with the Geico gecko.

It all adds to the story.

Despite the whirlwind of events, everything turned out okay. We were too naïve at the time to understand the real threats involved throughout the process of Luke's birth, but we later learned about how lucky we were—how abruptio placentae sometimes led to physical and mental deformities and sometimes death. My aunt Joann, actually, told us shortly after we brought Luke home that she had lost a child due to abruptio placentae. During the first week where we were visiting Luke, the OB nurse approached us and said, "I'm just really glad this worked out for you. You guys were fortunate."

The more we learned, the more fortunate we felt. The only bad news, really, was that we had to leave Luke at the hospital for several days because of all the blood he swallowed. And since our insurance wouldn't allow us to stay at the hospital for more than twenty-four hours, we had to leave Luke in the hands of doctors and nurses—all day, every day, for a week straight.

To cleanse his skin of the reptilian pigment, they put him under a light, as if in a laboratory, and made him wear tiny sunglasses with nickel-sized lenses. Poor Luke—our little lizard-child baking under a light in a diaper and shades, day-in and day-out. ✹

Though we expected that welcoming a child into this world would dramatically change our lives, it didn't for the first week. Our daily routines hardly changed. This was strange. Since it was a forty-minute drive to the hospital, I would go to work every day, get off at around five or six o'clock in the evening, pick up Lorri from home, and then we would drive to the hospital to see our son. Lorri's parents were staying at our house at the time to welcome Luke into our household, and when we kept showing up each evening empty-handed, I think they began to wonder what was going on.

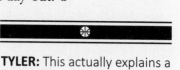

TYLER: This actually explains a lot about Luke now.

CODY: Hahahahahaha!!! Luke was a lizard!!!

One evening when we went to the hospital to make our daily visit to see our son, our doctor handed us a thick booklet of McDonald's gift certificates. Apparently, he knew the manager at McDonald's, and everything that transpired that day had become the talk of the town.

We dropped by McDonald's later that day to thank the manager for his kind gesture and apologize for the mess we made.

"Well, the baby started here," the manager laughed. "Consider it a baby present. Plus, you never got to finish your sandwich."

We still couldn't take our baby home, but at least we could eat at McDonald's whenever we wanted.

"If I ever get to take my baby home, I'm going to hold him until he is eighteen years old," I remember Lorri telling me.

That became difficult when Luke was eighteen years old and nearly seven feet tall.

Whenever Lorri was pregnant with Luke, I remember asking her, "Do you want a boy or a girl?"

"I don't care," she told me. "As long as it's healthy."

I paused before I asked my next question.

"But what if it's not healthy?" I asked.

We had never thought about this before. It was something neither of us had ever had to deal with in either of our families. Lorri's two brothers were healthy, and all eleven of my brothers and sisters were healthy. It led to a lengthy conversation as we considered the possibility that something unexpected *could* happen. What would we do? What would that mean? How would a circumstance like that change our lives? How would it affect our marriage? How would it affect us emotionally? Financially? Professionally?

We eventually came to the conclusion that the word "abortion" was something we would never even utter. It was something we would never allow into our minds.

Though I would not say I lived a life intertwined by faith in my early years of marriage (not that it wasn't important, it just wasn't at the core of my being), I couldn't help but think of my Catholic roots. My parents wouldn't even use contraceptives because of their faith in God and how they believed He would bless them with the number of children He wanted them to have. Not to say I agreed or disagreed with contraceptives, but as I thought about my family, I was, indeed, challenged by their mindset and outlook: They believed the Lord would give them whatever they could handle.

After Luke's birth, however, our eyes were opened to the reality that sometimes things don't go as you planned. And sometimes, these circumstances have the potential to change your life.

When Lorri was pregnant three years later with Tyler, our second child, we were no longer as naïve as we once were. Our naiveté with

Luke, in a way, saved us from not stressing out too much. I was very thankful to God for this. If we would have known all we know now, who is to say our panic and anxiety wouldn't have led to some poor decisions in the heat of the moment? Or maybe it would have led to more hesitation in the blur of the moment?

Because we were much more in touch with the possibility that things could go wrong the second time around, however, we naturally started talking about disabilities again. What if we weren't as lucky as we were with Luke? What if another issue arose throughout her pregnancy? What if an ultrasound revealed potential issues with the development of the fetus?

We once again arrived at the same conclusion, however: If we were *blessed* with a child with any sort of disability, then it must mean God felt we could handle it—just like He must have felt that my parents could handle twelve children on a farmer's salary. It was not an easy thing to believe, but, for some reason, though difficult to explain, it seemed to be the only thing that made sense.

I don't even like the phrase "if something goes wrong" when it comes to childbirth, because, if we approach the things of this life with the right attitude and mindset, I really do believe God can turn anything, even hardship or unexpected circumstances, into a tremendous *blessing*.

As Lorri was pregnant with Tyler, I tried not to get too worked up over everything that had unfolded in our past with Luke. Of course, it was a concern. It's not as if I ignored the near-tragedy that almost took place; I just didn't see what good worrying about it would do. It was beyond my control. If God can make good of any situation, why do we exhaust ourselves trying to control the uncontrollable? I don't know why bad things happen. I'm not sure if God allows them to happen or if everything is merely a byproduct of this cruel, fallen world, but the common thread in every good and bad circumstance seems to be the truth that God *can* work all things for the good of those who love Him (Romans 8:28). And knowing this and believing this has helped me free up my mind. It allowed us to look back and laugh about the McDonald's booth, railroad tracks, hospital construction, and our poor, little, spotted-lizard baby in sunglasses.

Everything is a new experience.

꧁꧂

As for our children's personalities, Luke is the outgoing one, and he couldn't wait to get into this world. He wouldn't even let me finish my food. He is also the more dramatic one, and nothing could have been more dramatic than both making an entire McDonald's restaurant aware of his arrival *and then* making me, Lorri, and her parents wait an entire week before we could take him home. ✲

Tyler, on the other hand, was the most introverted of all our children, and he was hesitant to ever enter this world. He was due on January 4, but he wasn't born until January 17, *two weeks* later. Knowing Tyler, his infant self was probably relaxing in Lorri's womb thinking along the logical lines of, "I'm perfectly happy here, so why would I leave?" ✲

LUKE: Dramatic? I'm not dramatic!

TYLER: Yes you are.

CODY: Yeah, you definitely are.

TYLER: True.

Lorri's parents had bought a plane ticket to visit our new California home in mid-January (I had accepted a position as a supervisor in a new Louis Rich plant, owned by Oscar Mayer), believing it would give Lorri and I some time to get settled in with our new baby. But when they arrived, there was no newborn baby to greet them. Her poor parents were probably thinking to themselves, "Here we go again." Though Lorri's parents always went out of their way to support us and be there for us, it didn't seem they were ever able to see our babies right after they were born.

As for Lorri, she was as pregnant as could be. I could have predicted Tyler would one day play in the NBA simply based on Lorri's size—even before she was nearly two weeks overdue. This sounds cruel, but she could actually put her dinner plate on her stomach instead of pulling out a television tray.

The doctors decided to induce labor the morning of January 17.

I woke up especially early that morning so I could buy some roses for Lorri. I knew she had grown increasingly nervous throughout

December and January because of what happened with Luke. She wondered if her abruptio placentae would return for this pregnancy, too; she wondered if she might run into a different issue. She struggled with the fact that, in two pregnancies, neither delivery seemed "normal." One was early. This one was late.

When Lorri woke up and saw the roses, she gave me a hug and started crying. This time, we didn't stop at McDonald's. There were no railroad tracks we had to cross on the way to the hospital. And there was no construction at all at the hospital. It was a much smoother start to delivery day.

We arrived at the hospital and the doctor gave her Pitocin, the inducing drug, and we walked up and down the hallway at the hospital waiting for the medicine to kick in, just talking. We always loved talking to each other.

When it finally came time for her to deliver the baby, I had fun analyzing the monitor. The baby would kick, and I would warn her about the coming contraction.

"Well, here comes another one," I'd say.

Then Lorri would make noises I hadn't heard in three years since Luke was born.

"Well, here comes another one," I'd say again.

I'm a nerd when it comes to technology so I really was amused by it all, and I was trying to make Lorri laugh and calm her down. Looking back, Lorri says I had way too much fun with the whole childbirth thing. Probably not the best time to crack jokes, I guess.

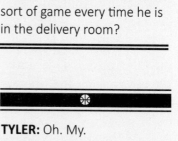

TYLER: Does Dad create some sort of game every time he is in the delivery room?

TYLER: Oh. My.

Finally, at ten o'clock in the morning on January 17, 1990, our little introvert, Tyler Paul Zeller, sharing my middle name, finally entered the world that terrified him. He was ten pounds, two and a half ounces, and twenty-two inches long. I had never seen a baby that big before. It was as if he was born as a two-month-old child. I already respected and adored Lorri, but I was absolutely in awe that she delivered a baby so large—and again she did it without the use of any epidural anesthetic.

He was much healthier than Luke, too. ✻

We called Lorri's parents from the hospital and told them that everything had gone well and they were welcome to bring Luke by to see his new, baby brother. When three-year-old Luke walked into the

TYLER: Some things never change.

room, wide-eyed and curious, Lorri turned and looked at me.

"Two of them," she laughed. "What have we done?"

From the very beginning, Lorri did a great job of making Luke feel proud that he was Tyler's older brother. She wanted to plant a seed in his mind early on that it's a *privilege* to be the older sibling and that Tyler would forever look up to him. I believe this fueled Luke's subconscious early on with the importance of being responsible, which helped him become a natural leader. ✻

From the very start, we tried to construct in him the idea of responsibility, which was an *opportunity* for him to lead. Luke knew there was always someone who would be watching him and admiring him.

LUKE: "From Lizard to Leader: The Story of Luke Zeller." Maybe a future memoir?

By the time Cody was born, a pattern had begun to develop. Luke was born when we lived in Iowa. Three years later, we moved to California, and Lorri became pregnant with Tyler. Three years later, we moved to Minnesota (when I accepted a position as a plant manager at Simmons Foods), and Lorri became pregnant with Cody. In conclusion, as I was continually transferred as I worked at various companies in the meat industry, each geographic change resulted in more Zeller spawn. ✻

Despite Luke's early arrival and Tyler's late arrival, Lorri's preg-

> ⬅ ✳
>
> **CODY:** Oh, so this is how babies are made!

nancy with Cody was as normal as could be. The night before her final appointment, she started having some minor contractions. She called the doctor the following morning at six o'clock and told him what had happened the night before. She just so happened to have an appointment that morning anyway, and the doctor told her to go to the emergency room if the contractions got worse; but if they didn't, she could just go to her appointment in a few hours, as scheduled.

She was fine throughout the morning, but on the way to her appointment, I made a dire mistake. I was hungry before her appointment, so, after dropping six-year-old Luke off at kindergarten and three-year-old Tyler off at a babysitter's, we went through the drive-thru for breakfast—the McDonald's drive-thru.

I should've known the golden arches were an omen around due dates. Lorri didn't even eat anything because she figured she might deliver that day.

We eventually arrived at her ten o'clock appointment, but her doctor wasn't there—he was at the hospital. Lorri's appointment was in the clinic, which was across town from the hospital.

"You can sit here," the nurse told us. "He will be over shortly."

"That's fine, not a problem," I said.

We sat down in the waiting room with all the other patients. The nurse eventually called Lorri's name and brought us into the examining room where we took a seat. This nurse was a business-like, organized lady, but she wasn't the most personable nurse we'd ever had. In our private conversations, Lorri and I started referring to her as "Nurse Ratched," referencing the nutty nurse in the film *One Flew Over the Cuckoo's Nest*.

"You can go ahead and change into your gown, if you'd like," she croaked, handing Lorri a hospital gown.

"All right," Lorri said, taking the gown.

"I'll be right back," she said in a monotone, crackly voice. "I'm going to go across the hall to get a cup of coffee."

"Sounds good," we told her.

The nurse closed the door behind her.

"She really loves her job," I said sarcastically.

Lorri stood up to start changing, and, right when she rose to her feet, her water broke. Actually, "exploded" is probably a better term than "broke."

I cannot explain it, but it was if Cody was already on his way out.

"Oh my gosh!" Lorri screamed. "I'm having this baby!"

I wasn't sure what to do. The examining room didn't even have any equipment to deliver a baby. There was only a table, sink, cabinet, and a couple of magazines. To top it all off, our doctor was in the delivery room in a different hospital on the other side of town. And Nurse Ratched had left to grab a cup of coffee.

"Go get someone!" Lorri screamed at me. I had completely frozen in shock.

I swung the door open and hurried down the hall, searching frantically to find someone.

I ran into a different nurse. Nurse Ratched was nowhere to be found.

"My wife is having a baby!" I told her, panting.

Within seconds, we were both in the examining room with Lorri. The nurse did a good job of remaining calm but eventually blurted, "Well, I need to go get the doctor!" And she bolted out the door.

Less than a minute later, she returned with another doctor from the practice.

The doctor entered the room.

He doesn't look like a doctor, I thought to myself. He wasn't dressed like a doctor, wasn't confident like a doctor, and, for some reason, he had a rag in his hand. He was also super negative.

"There's no way you're having the baby here," he said firmly. "We're not equipped to have a baby here."

Lorri shot him a glare as if to say, "Do you not see with your eyes what is happening right now?"

"We can't have a baby here," the doctor repeated.

"Look," Lorri said sternly in a heavy sweat, "we're having the baby *right here, right now.*"

The doctor grunted and left the room.

"Was that a janitor?" I said to Lorri.

"Steve," she grimaced, forcing a painful smile.

"I'm sorry," I said.

"I don't even care at this point," Lorri eventually said desperately. "The *janitor* can deliver this baby. JUST GET SOMEBODY IN HERE!"

Moments later, our doctor *finally* walked through our door and into the examining room. And again, much like the nurse who greeted us as I carried Lorri aimlessly around the hospital lawn when she was pregnant with Luke, the doctor similarly felt like an angel sent from above.

"Well," he said comfortably, analyzing the situation, "looks like we're having a baby."

A high school athlete had probably gotten his or her physical in that same examining room moments before, and here we were, *about to have a baby*. Certainly not how you picture everything happening.

Still, I had to help fuel Lorri with confidence.

"This is great," I told Lorri. "This is great. We're fine. This is great."

"We have *nothing* to have a baby!" Lorri snapped.

"We're good," I told her. "We're fine. This is great."

A different nurse entered the room. It soon became apparent that Nurse Ratched and Mr. Janitor must have been re-stationed elsewhere. This was comforting—I would have preferred Cheech and Chong over those two.

"Get some pads," the doctor told the nurse, taking control of the situation.

"Yes sir," she said, exiting the office.

The doctor proceeded to pile some sheets at the end of the table as a pillow, in case he struggled to hold onto the baby.

Ten minutes or so passed. The doctor had done a good job of giving us confidence that he had things under control, but sheer havoc was still unfolding all around us. I don't know how many times I said "this is great" and "breathe."

"Where is she?" the doctor said under his breath, referring to the nurse. I wasn't entirely sure what he wanted pads for, but I'm guessing they were to make Lorri more comfortable.

A few minutes later, the nurse returned.

The doctor looked up.

"What're those for?" the doctor said, confused.

I looked up at the nurse. She had an assortment of metallic pans clanking in her hands.

"You said you wanted pans," she said.

"No, *pads,*" he emphasized. *"Pads."*

"Oh my gosh," she said sheepishly, shuffling out of the room.

"I guess she thought we were boiling water," the doctor joked.

I chuckled.

Jokes are even funnier to me in unlikely places.

"Reminds me of the old westerns where they boiled water to make everything sterile," I told the doctor.

He laughed.

I laughed.

Lorri kept panting.

The nurse eventually returned with several pads, and the doctor propped Lorri up.

"Sorry about that," the nurse said, out of breath.

"You're fine," the doctor laughed.

Our new nurse, we would later find out, happened to teach a Lamaze class, so she was a huge help in her instruction of Lorri's breathing patterns.

"Don't push yet," she would tell Lorri gently. "All right, *now* push. Good. Good. You're doing good, Mrs. Zeller . . . Don't push . . . All right, now push. Good. Good."

The presence of Nurse Ratched's replacement and Mr. Janitor's replacement was calming Lorri and making her feel much more confident in the circumstances we were dealing with.

Then, in five minutes, just like that, Cody Allen Zeller was born. We gave him the middle name "Allen" after his Uncle Al, Lorri's brother. The date was October 5, 1992.

After delivering Cody, the doctor held him and said, "Yeah, looks healthy," as if he was inspecting a car engine.

"Well," he said casually, "we don't even have a scale to tell you how much the baby weighs."

The doctor handed Cody to me, as if he was testing out a bowling ball.

"What do you think?" the doctor said. "About nine pounds?"

"Yeah," I agreed, handing Cody back to the doctor, "about nine pounds."

He was probably about twenty-two inches long.

Lorri and I passed Cody back and forth for several minutes. I think we were both still in shock. I'm not sure if Lorri could even comprehend what had just happened.

In a normal situation, we would have been in the OB wing of the hospital. With our "contamination" (since he wasn't born in a sterile environment), we would have had to be separated with Cody going to the pediatrics wing and Lorri going to the surgery wing. However, we didn't want to be apart from Cody; plus, the doctor said he was perfectly healthy anyway.

Five or ten minutes passed.

"You know," the doctor said, "you guys are doing all right. The baby is doing just fine. If you want, you can just go home."

Lorri and I looked at one another, as if to say, "*That's it?*"

Cody's birth story fits his personality perfectly because he is such a "go with the flow" type of person. He doesn't need much to be happy, just as he didn't need all the proper equipment and procedures when he was born. Nothing is difficult to him. He enters a challenge, then simply passes through it.

I looked at the doctor and shrugged.

"Great, sounds good," I said.

"Come with me, and I'll get you a wheelchair," the doctor said to me.

I went with the doctor into the waiting room, and he gave me a wheelchair among some other things in a bag for Lorri and Cody. He shook my hand, laughed and told me it had been an interesting day, and then said that he had to go back to the delivery wing to see another patient.

"Thanks, Doc," I told him.

As I made my way back toward the examining room with the wheelchair, an older woman in the waiting room held the door for me.

"You must be the dad with the baby," she told me in a congratulatory way.

"I am, I am," I affirmed. "How'd you know?"

"Everyone in here knows about it," she said.

Apparently, the news had traveled through the clinic.

The older woman gave me a high-five, congratulating me.

I laughed and returned to Lorri in the examining room.

"You're a legend out there," I told Lorri. "The whole waiting room thinks this is awesome."

We put Lorri in a wheelchair and wheeled her past all the sick people in the waiting room. They stood up and applauded. ✺

Upon getting in the car, we realized it was lunchtime and went through the drive-thru again at the same McDonald's. As we pulled up to the window to pay for our meals, we realized it was the same girl who served us breakfast a few hours before. Lorri and I took bets

CODY: Got my first standing ovation ten minutes into this world and nothing has changed since. No big deal!

on whether or not she would notice it was us again. She handed us our food and did a double-take with her eyes.

"Weren't you guys here this morning?" she said, as if to make sure she wasn't going insane.

"Yep," I laughed.

"Nice," she said, somewhat confused as to why we were going to McDonald's twice in one day. "Where've you been?"

"Well, we had a baby," I said, pointing to Cody.

"Oh my goodness," she said, shocked.

When we returned home, our neighbors, ironically, had tied balloons to our basketball goal.

〜〜〜

When Cody was six months old, we moved from Minnesota to Washington, Indiana, as I accepted a position as a plant manager at Perdue Foods. Considering our geographic pattern, I figured Lorri would get pregnant again. Honestly, I would have kept going. I had eleven brothers and sisters, after all. I had no intentions of stopping—three children felt like nothing compared to the chaos I grew up with. But maybe the traumatic experiences of all three births had been enough for Lorri. When we moved to Indiana, she said to me,

"Why don't we just get a dog?"

So we did.

And we haven't had a child or moved to another state since. I suppose she figured out the pattern. If we wouldn't have gotten a dog, we may have ended up having twelve children in twelve different states. Who knows?

I was interviewed on the radio one time as the kids were starting to gain some attention for their basketball abilities, and the radio host said to me, "Well, I need to ask the question everyone is wondering: Why didn't you have more kids?"

"Well," I told him, "Lorri locked up the bull right after Cody was born and just never let the bull back out." ❁

That quote spread like a wildfire.

CODY: Awkward . . .

"Mom!" Cody yelled from his room.

I was almost asleep in my bedroom with Steve.

"Mauuuuuuuum!" Cody yelled again, in much more of a whine. I sighed.

"What's he want now?" Steve also whined.

"I don't know," I groaned, wiping my eyes.

"Mom!" Cody yelled again.

"Yes?" I yelled back to Cody.

"I wet the bed!" Cody yelled.

Cody was probably two and a half years old at the time. Steve and I were a bit frustrated he was still wetting the bed when his older brothers were both potty trained at two years old, but we were trying to be patient with him.

"All right, be there in a second!" I yelled to Cody, rising to my feet.

Steve rolled back over and fell asleep again.

I entered Cody's room, removed his sheets, threw them in the washer, and placed new sheets on his bed.

TYLER: That's embarrassing.

CODY: There's a method to the madness.

"Sorry," Cody said, shrugging helplessly, looking up at me with his little eyes.

It was the most adorable apology I had ever seen.

"It's okay, bud," I told him. "Now let's get some sleep."

Cody curled up next to me as I lay down in his bed.

"Good night, Mom," he said, falling asleep in my arms.

"Good night, bud," I told him.

A few nights later, I was once again about to fall asleep with Steve in our bedroom.

"Mom!" Cody yelled.

I opened my eyes.

"Mauuuuuuuum!" Cody yelled again.

"When is he gonna learn?" I said to Steve.

"No idea," Steve grunted, rolling over.

"Yes?" I yelled back to Cody.

"I wet the bed!" Cody yelled.

I sighed.

"I wet the bed!" Cody yelled again.

"All right," I said, "be there in a second."

I entered his room and repeated the routine. Remove the sheets. Throw them in the washer. Place new sheets on the bed. Fall asleep with Cody.

"Good night, Mom," Cody said. "I'm really sorry."

"It's okay," I said.

The following week, I was once again about to fall asleep in my bedroom. Steve had already passed out.

"Mom!" Cody yelled from his room.

"You've got to be kidding me," I muttered under my breath.

"Mauuuuuuuum!" Cody yelled again.

"Yes?" I yelled back to Cody.

"I wet the bed!" Cody said immediately.

Steve woke up.

"That's it!" he grunted, angrily.

Steve arose to his feet.

"What are you doing?" I worriedly asked.

"He keeps wetting the bed because he likes for you to go in his room and fall asleep with him," he told me.

I gave Steve a crazy look.

"He's not even three years old, Steve," I said.

"I'm well aware," Steve grunted, rolling his eyes. "And he's the most conniving toddler I've ever seen."

I gave Steve another crazy look.

"All right, you handle it, then," I said, rolling over.

"I will," he said, stomping into the hall.

"Be right there!" Steve yelled to Cody, leaving our room and marching down the hallway.

A few minutes later, Steve came back into our bedroom.

"What'd you do?" I said.

"I'm making him sleep on the wet bed," Steve said bluntly.

"Steve!" I said. "He's not a dog! He's a kid!"

"Don't worry, I made him change out of his pajamas."

"But what about his sheets?"

"He wet the left side of the bed. He's sleeping on the right side of the bed. I'm not changing those sheets until the morning. He is the one who wet the bed. He can deal with it."

"All right, all right," I said.

Over the next week, Cody didn't yell for me, and I started to believe Steve might have been right. Was Cody manipulating me? It was both twisted and brilliant. I couldn't believe the lengths his little mind would go to just to get whatever he wanted. He would wet the bed in an attempt to control people! He had me wrapped around his finger.

Then, one night, we heard Cody yelling again.

"Mom!" he yelled.

"Mauuuuuuuum!" he yelled again.

"You've got to be kidding me," Steve said.

"Steve, maybe he really is struggling with peeing the bed."

"Yeah, maybe you're right," Steve said.

"Yes?" I yelled to Cody.

There was a long pause.

"Is Dad awake?" Cody yelled.

Steve sat up and looked at me in absolute disbelief.

"He's awake now!" I yelled back.

There was another long pause.

Next thing we knew, all we heard was the *pat-pat* of Cody's little feet on the hardwood floor as he made his way down the hall. We heard him enter the bathroom, relieve himself, and flush the toilet. Lesson learned. ✱

LUKE: Why does this story not surprise me? This is the same kid that took my wallet on my wedding day and hid my license behind my insurance card. On my wedding day! I couldn't get my car out of valet parking at the hotel the next morning because I couldn't find my license.

TYLER: You never know what Cody is going to do. The only thing you *do* know is that he is always up to something. Once, he had these little firecrackers that popped when you pulled them apart. He put two of them on the kitchen cabinet and recorded Mom opening the cabinet. They popped, and Mom just about jumped out of her socks. Cody sent me the video while I was at UNC—I couldn't stop laughing.

TYLER: I guess Cody never got the memo?

It's vital that your children respect you by the time they are five years old. ❋

But the most difficult thing about earning their respect is that you have to punish them and discipline them. And the most difficult thing about punishing them and disciplining them is that they are so darn cute. Seriously! It's hard to discipline someone who is staring up at you and saying "sorry" with those adorable little eyes, even if the apology *is* a blatant, ridiculous lie. It's hard to punish someone that you love. Every time I hear "You're Gonna Miss This" by country artist Trace Adkins, I reflect back on the days when our boys were so small and adorable. Just thinking about how cute they were makes me wonder how we possibly managed to discipline them.

I hear a lot of parents joke around and say things along the lines of, "Oh, he runs the household" in reference to one of their children because of how cute he or she is. It's not too harmful whenever a five-year-old is "running the household" and you give him whatever he wants, but it becomes harmful when a fifteen-year-old is running the household. That's when you have problems.

Big problems.

Parents must be parents.

Why do we, as parents, hesitate to be parents when children don't hesitate to be children? They will naturally disobey. They will naturally try to get everything they can from you. Cody, for example, purposefully wet the bed just to get me to sleep in his room with him.

Parents must continue to be parents throughout their children's teenage years, as well.

When we lived in California, a friend of mine had a daughter who was a senior in high school. She gave her daughter freedom, but the main rule she had to abide by was her midnight curfew. If she missed her curfew, then she had to miss the next thing on her schedule. It was as clear as day.

One night, her daughter was out with her boyfriend on a Friday evening watching a movie at the nearby theater. The movie went longer than they expected, and the daughter didn't walk into her house until twelve thirty, a half hour past her curfew. She was in trouble. And the consequence was that she had to miss the next thing on her schedule.

The next thing on her calendar was her senior prom on Saturday evening, the very next day.

What do you do in a situation like that? If you are the parents, you've already spent money on her dress, and, not only that, you probably *want* her to attend her senior prom.

But what is the rule? Does it say, "Does not apply the night before prom" in fine print at the bottom? It appears to be a lose-lose situation. If you make her stay home, you appear heartless. If you let her go, you appear weak. However, if you, as a parent, have done a good job of clearly defining the rule, then it cannot be your fault if your child breaks it. Consistency is the key.

One Sunday when Cody was a senior in high school, our phone started ringing off the hook because it was revealed that Cody had been named Indiana Mr. Basketball, the most prestigious hoops award in the state.

"So what are you guys going to do to celebrate?" one of our friends asked Steve over the phone.

"I'm not real sure," Steve said. "Cody is outside mowing the lawn right now."

"Mowing the lawn?" our friend questioned. "He just won Mr. Basketball!"

"I know," Steve said, "but Cody knows one of the chores he has to complete every weekend is to mow the lawn. He waited until Sunday to mow. He has to get it done before dark. Then we can go out and celebrate."

See, kids already have friends and siblings and teachers and coaches. But what they *need* is a parent. So it is important to be one. If you are a parent to your children from the start—even if it's difficult, even if you have to make them sleep in a wet bed or stay home from prom or mow the lawn before you celebrate a Mr. Basketball award—it allows you to be a friend to your children down the road. Being friends with your children is more enjoyable than disciplining them, but disciplining them must come first.

Now, other times, it's just the opposite. You don't find their actions cute at all. Instead, their actions infuriate you, and it takes every bit of restraint not to lash out at them based on your own emotion.

Regarding our children, the angriest I've ever become was when Tyler was a fifth grader playing Little League baseball.

Now, if you need to know one thing about Tyler, it's this: He is always in his own little world. And he's always been like that. When he was younger, he was always playing with Legos alone in his room or going around the house acting like he was a ninja.

TYLER: Really? After all of your arguments with Luke, *I'm* the one that made you most angry? I always minded my own business!

The day I was angered the most happened when Tyler was playing Little League as a fifth grader. I remember him coming downstairs after he had spent all day doing who knows what up in his room.

"Mom," he said, "I have baseball practice right now."

"No, honey, it doesn't start until five o'clock," I said.

"I know, but Coach changed it."

I stopped what I was doing and looked at him.

"He changed it?"

"Yeah," he said, "I just now remembered."

"All right, get in the car," I said, hurriedly trying to get organized.

We hopped in the car and sped to the baseball diamond. I hated when our kids were late to athletic events because it demonstrated a lack of responsibility.

"Tyler, you *have* to let me know whenever your coach changes something," I told him.

"I know," he said dismissively.

I scratched my head out of frustration.

We eventually arrived at the baseball diamonds, and, to my dismay, there wasn't a single car in the parking lot.

"Tyler?" I said, as if to demand an answer.

"Oh yeah," he remembered, slowly piecing everything together. "Practice got switched to the sports complex. It got switched from five to four thirty, and from the elementary fields to the sports complex," he recited, as if remembering exactly what his coach had said at the end of the previous practice.

"All right," I murmured, making a U-turn and heading down a different street toward the direction of the sports complex.

I didn't say anything on the way. He already knew I was upset. It wasn't worth it.

Ten minutes later (it was probably five o'clock by now, already a half hour into practice), we pulled up to the sports complex baseball fields. Tyler quickly opened his door, then popped open the trunk to grab his mitt.

"Mom?" he said from behind the car.

"Yeah?" I answered.

"I forgot my glove."

You've got to be kidding me.

I snapped.

"Dang it, Tyler," I said. "Get in the car."

He got back in the car, and we made our way *back* toward the house to get his glove so we could go *back* to the baseball diamond. I knew by the time we made it to the fields for a second time, they would already be *at least* forty-five minutes or an hour into practice.

All the way home, I lectured him.

"Tyler, you *have* to be more responsible," I told him. "Whatever your coach says to the team, you *have* to tell me. How do I know if you don't tell me? And you need to make a checklist. Don't get in the car unless you know you have everything for practice. By the way, how do you forget to bring your baseball glove to baseball practice? You have to focus more, Tyler. You have to be responsible."

I looked over at Tyler. We were flying down Indiana country roads, and he was simply looking out the window, in a daze.

"Tyler," I said.

He didn't say anything.

"Tyler!" I said again, very sternly.

Still, he didn't say anything.

"Mom?" he said, in a questioning tone.

"Yes?" I said.

Tyler pointed toward something outside. He was in his own little world.

"How far apart do you think those telephone poles are?" ✹

I was so shocked and infuriated, I'm not sure if I said anything at all. Tyler was oblivious to the situation.

TYLER: What? It's a fair question!

〰〰

Now, if you thought that was ridiculous, look no further than Tyler's little brother. The maddest Steve has ever been with our children had to do with Cody when he was three.

(By the way, our arsenal of "Cody stories," oddly, seem to take place when he was three years old. To give you an accurate depiction of the way Cody was at that age, I remember Cody and I once going to the bank when he was three, and he asked me if he could get some candy from the teller since the local bank always had a jar of candy. I told him "no" and he replied, "Well, if I smile, I can get anything I want.") ✹

This particular incident with Steve took place on a pretty typical weekday evening while Luke was at soccer practice. To give me a little

⇐ ✿

CODY: Marketing 101.

bit of alone time at the house, Steve took Cody and Tyler to the soccer fields to pick up Luke.

Practice, however, had gone longer than expected, so after thirty minutes of sitting in the car, Steve got out of the car to stand in the parking lot and get some fresh air and talk to some of the parents.

While Steve was standing outside, Cody and Tyler apparently came up with some sort of game in the car. Our boys seemed to make a game or competition out of *everything*. They were jumping on the front seats, hitting their heads on the car ceiling, and laughing afterward. Boys.

Steve swung open the driver's side door. "What are you guys doing?" he said to them, as they jumped, hit their heads on the ceiling, and started laughing again.

"Stop it," Steve told them. "Someone is going to get hurt."

Steve closed the door and returned to a conversation he was having in the parking lot.

They didn't stop.

They kept jumping.

And the next time Steve looked at the car, he noticed that the entire front windshield was cracked. Cody had apparently continued jumping on the seat, leapt forward too much, and, instead of hitting his head on the ceiling, rammed his little, rock-hard skull into the glass. Instead of a *thump*, I imagine there was a *crack*.

His head must have struck the windshield perfectly, because the entire glass had spider-webbed. Cody, somehow, was perfectly fine, sitting quietly in the passenger seat, probably fearing his father's coming wrath. ✿

Steve was so livid that he knew if he remained in the same fifty-foot radius of Cody, he would probably act out of anger, so he paced around the parking lot attempting to cool off. Right at that time, Luke was approaching the car from the soccer fields, carrying his soccer bag.

TYLER: When it happened, I had two questions running through my mind: "Why did Cody do that?" and "What is Dad going to do?"

"Whoa!" Luke exclaimed. "What happened to the windshield?"

"Not a good time, Luke," Steve said. "Not a good time."

As comical as the stories are, the point is that, just as it is important to be consistent in making your children uphold the rules, we learned that it's also important to be consistent in how you punish your children for not upholding the rules.

The point of punishing your children is to *teach* them what they did wrong, not to take out your anger on them for whatever stupid thing it was that they did wrong. Teaching them that there are consequences must trump your own emotion and/or rage. Why? Because, just as failing to deliver the consequences of breaking a rule demonstrates weakness (the prom story), so does overdoing the consequences whenever they break a rule. Consistency produces predictability, and predictability is important. As parents, we never wanted our children to think that we were emotional time bombs. But, again, this is difficult because, to put it bluntly, sometimes the things they do are beyond belief.

So how can consistency be attained? First of all, I think *simplicity* is important: If you do (fill in the blank), then (fill in the blank) will happen. Basic math. In Steve's household growing up, it was an understood rule that if one of the twelve children got in trouble during the day—whether it was with his mother or at school—then he or she would have to confess the crime to the entire family at dinner time. To avoid this embarrassment in front of the family, humiliation in front of their father, and the consequences their father would deliver, the solution was to avoid getting in trouble. It was a pretty simple system. And it was predictable.

The rules in our household in which we raised Luke, Tyler, and Cody were similar:

- *Rule No. 1: Don't do anything that would cause me to wake up Steve.*
- *Rule No. 2: If you have any questions, refer to Rule No. 1.*

The underlying value to this was respect. Steve was working fifty to sixty-hour workweeks, so it taught the boys to be respectful and conscientious of the fact that Steve needed to sleep if he wanted to pay the bills for our family. And, in order to be respectful of Steve, they had to respect me. If I had to wake Steve up over something one of them did, it wasn't respectful to either of us.

This brings me to my second point: *teamwork*. The boys knew that if they did something wrong, it wasn't just between me and the boys or Steve and the boys. Rather, it was between *us* and the boys. They knew Steve and I were a team. If they did something that I viewed as disrespectful, it didn't just involve me disciplining them, it involved waking up Steve so we would both discipline them.

One day, when Luke was in junior high, he stomped into our sun-room where Steve was relaxing and watching television. I think Luke and I had just been in an argument. (Luke and I, for whatever reason, had more fights than I had with both Tyler and Cody combined.)

"You gotta talk to Mom," Luke told Steve.

"Well, why is that?" Steve said.

"She's just being really unreasonable," he said.

Steve started laughing. "I ain't talking to your mom," he said. "She's in charge, and whatever she says, you have to respect that."

"Yeah, but she's so unreasonable," he said again. (We also think he had just learned the word "unreasonable.")

"You talk to her, Luke," Steve said. "I'm not talking to her."

"But you agree, right?" Luke said to Steve, as if believing that the only reason why Steve didn't want to talk to me was because he agreed with Luke.

"Yeah, of course," Steve said as Luke threw up his hands and breathed a sigh of relief. "I agree with your mom," Steve continued. "Whatever she says, goes." ✪

Luke shrieked through his gritted teeth, and he stomped out of the room.

Overall, consistency was attained in our household because our children knew Steve and I were on the same team. Whatever Steve said was

LUKE: For some reason, I always thought I could get Dad on my side in my conflicts with Mom, but it never worked.

the law. Whatever I said was the law. Our children could not use either of us as a loophole to get around the law. Children will naturally try to divide and conquer in rebellion, so it makes logical sense for parents to remain a team in how they handle their children's actions.

Anytime Steve or I disagreed with each other in parenting (and believe me, there were plenty of disagreements), we would talk to one another in private. Until we were behind closed doors, we defended each other's words and actions. When we had parenting disagreements, the end goal was to make each other better parents, not to prove how one person was right or wrong. Pridefully, as humans, our natural desire is to try and win a conflict. However, as a team, the end goal must be the betterment of each individual.

It's no surprise that Steve and I sometimes handled things in different ways. Steve and I, though we are one, have different personalities and come from different backgrounds. This leads to my next point. When it comes to consistency, I think the important thing to remember is that there isn't a set formula. Each child is different. Each parent is different. Don't be afraid to *be creative* throughout your consistency. Parents can use different means (creativity) to demonstrate the same themes (consistency).

When the kids were young, I remember going on a family vacation to Illinois to meet up with my parents. The real treat for the kids was that we were staying in a hotel, and that meant that they got to swim in the hotel pool. They probably still have chlorine in their skin for how much time they spent in hotel pools in their childhood. In an effort to make sure our children didn't walk away from vacation with lifetime chemical burns, one day we decided to take them to the Miller Park Zoo in Bloomington, Illinois.

The zoo had an area where we could walk around and pet baby wallabies. The most comical thing about this experience was that Cody, at two or three years old, stood at the exact same height as the baby wallabies. ❂

I can still picture Cody standing face-to-face with one of the wallabies, looking into its eyes, and studying it as if it was from outer space. Part of me wondered if the

CODY: I'm three years old in all of these stories! Best year of my life.

wallaby was going to jackrabbit kick him in the chest.

Instead, they just looked at one another.

What we didn't know at the time was that this incident actually ended up really scarring Cody emotionally. When we returned home to Indiana, Cody's mind started running wild when he lay in bed at night. He started to believe there were kangaroos in his bedroom.

One night, Steve and I were watching television in the living room after the kids had gone to bed, and Cody came running down the stairs.

"What are you doing out of your room?" Steve said to Cody.

"Kangaroos!" he said, as if he were fleeing from an entire army of them.

Steve turned and whispered to me, "Get the video camera." (There are some moments that simply must be captured.) �֍

Cody hopped onto Steve's lap.

"What's going on, buddy?" Steve said.

"There are . . . there are . . . kangaroos in my room," Cody said softly.

> **LUKE:** This is probably one of my favorite home videos.

"Kangaroos?"

"Yeah."

"How do you know?"

"I-I-I heard them," Cody said.

"What did they sound like?"

"Like this: *crckkkkkkkk,*" he said, demonstrating a scratching noise.

"Hmmmmm," Steve said, "are you sure?"

"Yeah!" Cody affirmed. "It sounded like *crckkkkkkkk.*"

Cody paused. "Can I sleep with you guys tonight?" he said.

"No," Steve laughed. "But I think I know what the sound was," Steve said gently.

"What was it?" Cody said, genuinely curious.

"I think it was just Dexter," Steve said, referring to our poodle.

"Dexter?" Cody questioned. You could see Cody's little mind working as he tried to connect the dots and discover whether or not it could be Dexter.

"Yeah, just Dexter. Sometimes he scratches the door with his paws."

"Dexter?" Cody said again, almost in disbelief.

"Yeah, Dexter," Steve said affirmatively.

Cody's eyes lit up, as if it suddenly made perfect sense.

"It was just Dexter!" Cody agreed, excitedly.

"Just Dexter," Steve smiled.

Creativity.

Not to oversimplify something as complex as parenting, but, when it came to discipline and punishment, we raised our children much like we raised our dog/wallaby, Dexter. ❋

When Dexter was a puppy, we were incredibly strict with him. If he had an accident in the house, we gently hit him with a newspaper and held his nose directly above his puddle of urine; if he ate something off the dinner table, we put him in his kennel; if he barked in the house, we punished him by putting

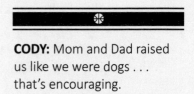

CODY: Mom and Dad raised us like we were dogs . . . that's encouraging.

him outside (in case you are skimming, I am talking about our family dog now, not Cody). We taught Dexter very early on the difference between right and wrong and what was acceptable and what was unacceptable by our family's standards. We knew that if we coddled Dexter just because he was a cute puppy, he would turn out to be a nightmare of a dog.

Conceptually, we did this same thing with our children. It didn't matter how cute they were, we knew that if we weren't hard on them at the beginning, they would try to run the house when they were older. Throughout parenthood, there is a progression from strict to trust—we were strict and sometimes harsh with our children early on, and we trusted them as time went on *if* they earned our trust.

One of the tools we used to discipline our children when they were younger was a timeout chair. Once, when Cody was sent to the timeout chair (probably when he was three), he tried to crawl away and sneak off somewhere. I caught him.

"Cody Allen Zeller!" I snapped, catching him in the act.

He looked at me wide-eyed, stopping right in his tracks.

"Get back in that chair, Mister," I said firmly, pointing at the chair.

He smiled and quietly crawled back into his chair. I joined Steve in the other room and told him, "That was the cutest thing I've ever seen."

The point is that we kept our truest emotions to ourselves and expressed them to one another in private in an effort to remain consistent and make sure our children upheld the rules of our household. When they were younger, we didn't grant them a ton of leniency. We took discipline very seriously early on, even though it was sometimes tough and exhausting.

The purpose behind being hard on them when they are young is to help ingrain in them what is right and wrong and ultimately help them start to develop their worldview at the earliest stage in life. I return to my analogy with Dexter. By the time Dexter was two years old, he immediately felt guilty if he had an accident in the house, ate something off the dinner table, or barked in the house. Why? Because he understood what was right and wrong. Dexter would wallow in his guilt, so grieved by the fact he disobeyed his owners and knew better than his actions indicated. He was so disappointed in himself that he hardly even needed a punishment. The guilt he felt became more of a punishment than our discipline. The emotion trumped the physical.

This goes back to "the Zeller name" concept Steve addressed at the start of the book. Because we raised our children on a firm foundation of right and wrong, the enjoyment of bringing honor to the Zeller name far trumped their desire to rebel against it. Luke, Tyler, and Cody will tell you that, as they grew older, doing drugs or sleeping around never seemed to be an option to them. It's not that these things aren't pleasurable (sin is pleasurable, after all, for a short while), it's just that doing these things never seemed to enter the forefront of their minds. They just knew that was not how someone with the Zeller name should act. They trusted that the way they were raised was much more fulfilling than going against it. ✹

LUKE: This is really true. As I got older and older, participating in some of the things my friends were doing, like underage drinking or partying, was never really a temptation simply because I knew that was not how someone with the Zeller name should conduct himself. I think I can speak for Tyler and Cody, too. When you already know the right way to live, why would you venture outside of those boundaries?

What it reminds me of is our relationship with God. One of the essentials to obeying God is truly believing that His way is better for us and it is in His will where we feel most free. Why do we sin if it is only going to harm us? Why would we walk down our own road if we know it's not going to lead us anywhere? At the heart of it, this is why Adam and Eve sinned: Ultimately, they believed their way was better. However, they eventually found out their way was much worse because of the consequences and pain they endured due to their separation from God. This is the theme throughout the entire Old Testament.

God doesn't tell us to avoid certain things because He is on some sort of a power trip or because He wants to rob us of life. He wants us to live better lives and experience and enjoy Him more. It's that simple. Much like parenting, His way helps us live better lives.

It is a fulfilling thing when your children eventually realize that everything that was established within the framework of your household was created to help them live better lives.

When Luke was playing in the NBA, he had a conversation with one of his teammates on a day they received their paychecks. His teammate explained to him how some of the paycheck went to the mother of one of his children, some of it went to the mother of another one of his children, and some of it went to the mother of another one of his children. The rest, he explained, was all his.

"What about you?" the player asked Luke. "How many of your kids' moms do you have to pay before you see any of that check?"

Luke, somewhat caught off guard, explained to him that he was married and didn't have any children.

"You didn't have any children before you were married?" the player asked.

"I got married as a virgin," Luke said.

The player couldn't believe it and, initially, actually thought that he was joking.

"I lost my virginity in seventh grade!" the player exclaimed.

I tell this story, not to paint Luke and his wife, Hope, as angels, but to remind you of the culture parents are up against and why it is so crucial to lead your children to a point where they can realize and believe that the straight and narrow isn't just the way their parents want them to live but it is the *better* way for them to live. Sometimes, unfortunately, this is something they have to figure out for themselves, much like how God grants us free will to experience what life is like without Him in order for us to realize how much we *need* Him.

This leads to another idea. Just as it is important to discipline your children (I suggest early on in their lives), it is just as important to eventually trust your children. Demonstrate your trust in them early, too. They may be more willing to obey if they don't feel like you are always trying to control.

In the process of moving from Minnesota to Indiana, we stayed in a hotel during the transition period. Cody was six months old, Tyler was three, and Luke was six. Steve and I needed to go over some of the paperwork for the house we just closed on in Minnesota and our new mortgage in Indiana. We needed about twenty minutes without the kids just so we could focus on all of the papers, discuss a few things, and make sure we did everything correctly.

We gathered the kids around and whispered to them, as if they were on a top-secret mission, "We're going to go down the hallway and fill out some paperwork. While we're gone, don't let anybody in the room."

We wanted them to feel like they were in charge. We wanted to give them responsibility.

"So when we come back," I whispered, "the password is 'Batman.' If someone knocks and doesn't get the password right, don't let them in."

They nodded. There was an excitement in their eyes that they were going to be in their own hotel room alone without their parents. They were taking the task we had given them very seriously.

In all actuality, we just sat in the hallway—if something horrible happened we would hear it. But they didn't know this, and twenty minutes later, when we had the paperwork completed, we "returned."

Steve knocked on the door of our hotel room.

We could hear their feet shuffling on the other side as they all ran to the door.

"What's the password?" they said.

"Let's test them," I whispered to Steve.

Steve nodded.

"Robin?" I said.

We could hear their little whispers on the other side. They didn't know what to say since we got the password wrong.

Eventually, Tyler spoke up: "Say 'Batman' and we'll let you in."

⁙⁙⁘

Just as failing to discipline your children will lead them to running the house, failing to trust your children will lead them to leaving the house. Again, this is the progression that took place within our household—from strict discipline (very little trust) to discipline intertwined with trust (you trust them the more they prove they can be trusted) to total trust (very little discipline).

If trust is never exhibited, the home environment becomes a place where children feel as if their parents are constantly nagging them or continually striving to control them. The result is that they eventually leave the house and search for alternate means of escaping. If your children do not feel comfortable in their own home, it's important to ask yourself why. Could it be because you never moved past the "strict discipline" stage? Could it be because they don't feel like you trust them? ✽

When Steve and I were dating, it was decided one Christmas that Steve would come out to Colorado with my family. He had never been out west before. Since we were leaving early the next morning to drive from Iowa to Colorado, Mom suggested that Steve stay at our place so we could leave directly from our house. With three bedrooms upstairs, there was plenty of room in the house, so it made sense for him to stay. However, when we returned to my parents' house that

> **CODY:** Throughout high school, our house is where I felt safest.

evening after going out for a movie, we noticed that my parents had made a bed for Steve on our old, worn-down, living room sofa downstairs.

All throughout the night, as Steve tried to sleep, the sofa cushions kept sliding out from underneath him. He eventually ended up sleeping on the cold, hardwood floor and only got a couple hours of sleep before a grueling road trip out west.

I was upset with my parents about that one. There was an extra bedroom upstairs that Steve could have slept in, but to me, they didn't even trust us enough to let us sleep on the same story of the house! Honestly, it made me feel like they didn't think very highly of me and my ability to make good decisions. They did a good job of trusting me in other situations, and fortunately, that feeling of insignificance never became a trend; but for some children, this does become a continual feeling. And consequently, because a child feels like his or her parents don't trust them to make good decisions, they will lash out by making bad decisions. It is a helpless feeling for a child to feel like he or she cannot do anything right. Trust, on the other hand, empowers them. They say the best leaders are the ones who can instill confidence in those below them. This is what parenting becomes—giving your children confidence to live their own lives and make wise decisions.

If your children don't feel like they have the freedom to live their own lives, then they most likely will not confide in you since they are trying to get away from you. And if they don't feel comfortable talking to you about the big things in life, then where will they turn? The Internet. Search engines. Or perhaps their own curiosity.

Search engines, specifically, have become the means in which we solve all of life's problems. Parents, essentially, aren't the supreme giver of knowledge anymore when it comes to their children. If parents don't talk to their children, or if children don't feel comfortable to talk to their parents, they can get the answer through plenty of alternative, less personal, and sometimes less awkward routes. And all it takes is for one of your children to Google "sex" for the most grotesque, offensive images to suddenly be at their fingertips.

Our first experience with discussing the "birds and the bees" with our children came on one Easter Sunday when Luke was nine, Tyler was six, and Cody was three. ✻

We allowed them to let our pet bunnies, Bubba and Fluffy, loose in the house, which we hardly ever allowed them to do. When we let them free on that infamous Easter Sunday, however, Bubba and Fluffy "connected" for the entire family to see. That was an interesting introduction to reproduction. ✻

Of course, we revisited the "birds and the bees" talks with each of our children several years after the Bubba/Fluffy incident. We didn't overwhelm them with these talks, but

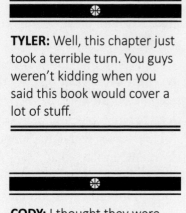

TYLER: Well, this chapter just took a terrible turn. You guys weren't kidding when you said this book would cover a lot of stuff.

CODY: I thought they were dancing.

we at least wanted them to know that they could talk to us about anything. Cody remembers Steve coming out into the sunroom when he was in middle school and bluntly saying to him, "So, Mom said you heard about sex."

"Uh, yeah, I heard something about it," Cody said awkwardly.

"Well, if you have any questions, just ask me," Steve said.

"All right," Cody grinned uncomfortably.

"I'd rather have you learn it from me than one of your buddies from school."

Luke, Tyler, and Cody, at one point or another, all confided in us about some of these "taboo" subjects as they got older. Each time, we made sure that we weren't surprised or shocked by the things they were telling us because we wanted them to continue coming to us for advice. Any type of emotion or overreaction to these things can make the home feel unsafe to your children. Rather, we treated the details they were telling us as "normal," but then used our conversation as an opportunity to give them practical advice and sharpen their worldview.

The goal of every parent must be for their household to become a safe haven to talk about anything and everything, as you move from strict discipline to trust. Trust is the tool that, ironically, gives your children the confidence to *also* trust in you as a parent.

I will never forget the day that I was taught one of the most humbling, valuable lessons a parent can ever learn—to learn from your children. ✳

Luke was in sixth grade, and we were on our way back from an AAU tournament in Fort Wayne, Indiana. Because Luke was already so tall (he was six foot four at the time and six foot nine by the time he was an eighth grader), he had already begun to receive an uncanny amount of attention from the basketball world, even in middle school.

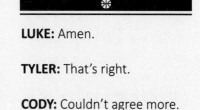

LUKE: Amen.

TYLER: That's right.

CODY: Couldn't agree more.

As he kept growing . . . and growing . . . and growing throughout his adolescent years, I'm not sure if any of us knew how to handle it.

Several AAU teams were recruiting him. After analyzing our options, we decided that a team and a coach out of Fort Wayne in northern Indiana was the best fit for him and best opportunity for him to improve as a player. I don't think Luke cared where he played. He just wanted to play basketball. He loved it.

It was a big commitment, though. Most Fridays, I would pack our car in the morning, go to work at Perdue Foods, leave work early to pick Luke up from school, then make a four-hour trip from our home in Washington to Fort Wayne to get him there in time for his first game on Friday night.

We would stay at a hotel on Friday, play three games on Saturday, stay in the hotel again on Saturday night, and then play in the tournament on Sunday until we were eliminated. It was usually just Luke and me while Lorri stayed in Washington with Tyler and Cody, as we juggled the schedules of three boys.

This particular Sunday, Luke's team happened to lose in the second game of the tournament. As we drove home, I was dissecting each game and possession, asking Luke why he did this or that, challenging some of his responses, and correcting the things he had done wrong.

"Remember, Luke, when a shot goes up, you *have* to find someone to box out," I'd tell him.

Then I'd inform him on some of the stats I gathered.

"On Sunday's game, the opposing team had five offensive rebounds while you were on the floor. This led to eight points. You guys lost by six."

Then I'd remember something else I noticed during a particular game.

"You started to fall back into your old habits on your free throw shooting, too, as the game winded down. Did you notice that? Were you nervous?"

Then I'd be reminded of something else. And I would go on and on and on, focusing on the road ahead of me, occasionally looking over at Luke, and sifting through all the thoughts I had gathered from the weekend.

This was our routine: Prepare for the weekend on the way up to Fort Wayne, analyze the weekend on the way back down.

About an hour outside of Washington, we stopped to grab a bite to eat at a McDonald's in Spencer, Indiana. I parked the car, turned it off, and looked over at Luke. He did not look at me. He simply stared out the front windshield blankly, his eyes fogged up and watery. ✸

"Dad," he said quietly, "was there anything I did *right* this weekend?"

That's when I realized: I had chewed him out for three consecutive hours.

LUKE: I felt overwhelmed, defeated, and crushed.

His words stung. I don't remember what my reaction was, but, knowing me, I probably grunted, spit, and sputtered, "You know, there are some things you did right."

I doubt I apologized, but neither of us said a word the remainder of the trip home. I'm sure he could tell his question left an impression on me. The last hour of the drive felt like five.

Luke's words were the only thing I could think about. They haunted me. The hurt in Luke's eyes and despair in his voice were impossible for me to simply ignore. For the rest of the trip, I stepped back and asked myself some difficult questions.

Why did I feel like I had to correct everything he did? Why was I being so hard on him? What good did it do? How were these weekly car rides from Fort Wayne to Washington *possibly* demonstrating that I loved him? Why was I treating everything from that weekend as if it were a life-or-death situation?

I began wrestling with a phrase that I believe every mother or father willing to become a better parent must adopt: *Maybe I'm wrong.* Socrates says, "An unexamined life is not worth living," and this couldn't be truer for parenting. We must continually remove ourselves from the situation (and the emotions that come with the situation) and analyze our actions.

But why was I doing what I was doing? What was taking place in my heart and mind that was ultimately leading to dealing with Luke the way I was?

I was reminded of a time I was talking to Luke's AAU coach after practice while Luke was shooting hoops. Luke approached his coach while we were talking, positioned his hands on the ball, and told him, "You told me to adjust my shot like this, and it has helped me a lot."

I noticed Luke's form was *exactly* what I had been telling him for months.

"Luke," I said, "that's what I've been telling you all along." ✸
Luke shrugged and went back to shooting.

"What difference does it make?" his coach asked me.

I looked at him. "Excuse me?" I said.

LUKE: I think I just tuned Dad out sometimes because he gave me so much advice. I wanted to do the things Dad was saying, but it became overwhelming. I would try to create a to-do list in my mind while he talked to me, but it felt like I always ran out of ink because the to-do list was several pages long.

"What difference does it make?" he repeated. "That *you* have to tell him?"

I didn't say anything.

"You wanted him to make sure he knew that the advice came from you," he continued, confronting me. "You did that for yourself. But what difference does it make? As long as he learns it, that's all you're after, right?"

It was tough to swallow, but he was right. *I was doing it for myself.*

This, I think, was one of the driving forces behind why I was dealing with Luke the way I was on the way back from Fort Wayne, too. I wanted him to do well so *I* could be proud. I wanted him to do well so people would say, "That's Steve Zeller's son out there." I wanted his play on the court to be a direct reflection of all *I* had taught him.

I was doing it for me. I was wrong.

Sometimes, it becomes too much about the *parent,* but other times, it also becomes too much about the *performance.* As I wrestled with all of this on the way home from Spencer, I realized I was guilty of focusing too much on Luke's performance, as well.

Everyone seemed to be raving about how tall Luke was, and I suppose my imagination went a little crazy. I wanted results. I wanted him to excel. Ultimately, I guess I was trying to push him into something—basketball—because I saw his potential. I feel so foolish looking back at the situation because I was criticizing a *sixth grader* for all kinds of things, failing to recognize that becoming a better basketball player is a process. I wanted him to get from Point A to Point D and skip Points B and C.

As parents, there is an internal struggle of desperately wanting your children to be better than yourself and better than the way they are currently acting or performing. This is not a bad desire. However, it becomes dangerous whenever this desire leads to controlling your children. This control leads to pushing your children too hard, which can sometimes result in settling for nothing less than perfection, which sometimes leads to your children's imploding and eventually quitting. You have to let your kids go through the process, whatever it may be, even if there are mistakes along the way.

I flash back to my own playing days and remember when my coach would sometimes ask me to do something. I would ask, "Why?" and he would respond, "Because I'm the coach, and you're the player." Sometimes, I took this concept too far in the way I instructed my children in the realm of athletics. Truth is, I *wasn't* Luke's coach. I was Luke's dad. My role was to support him in basketball more than instruct him, to love him despite his performance.

Performance-based love from parents produces performance-based identities in their children. Studies have actually proven that even telling your children something positive along the lines of, "You're a good basketball player," can actually have a detrimental effect on them because their entire identity is based on their performance. Therefore, whenever they have a day when they are a bad basketball player, they will consequently feel worthless and empty. It's far too easy to hook a kid's identity to what they are doing or what they have done. That is why I love the idea of implementing character into *everything* because you hook their identity to something much more long-lasting and important than their performance.

It's more of a comical story, but I'm reminded of a time when Luke was playing Little League baseball in fourth or fifth grade. He was hit by a pitch during a game, which made him extremely timid at every at-bat that followed. Every time the pitcher wound up, he would immediately step away from the pitch out of fear.

So, one day, I decided to take him out in the back yard and teach him that there was plenty of time to move away, even from a pitch that was heading right toward his head. I started throwing soft, T-balls at him, as he dodged each one. To this day, Luke swears they were baseballs. ❀

In his mind, I'm sure they were.

LUKE: They were!

Either way, there was plenty of time for him to move.

Luke, obviously, didn't like the drill, and he threw his bat down and stormed into the house. Lorri was in the kitchen working on something.

"Dad's lost his mind!" Luke said to Lorri, flustered and upset.

"What?" she said.

"Dad's lost his mind," Luke repeated. "He's throwing baseballs at me."

"Now, why would he do that?" she laughed. Luke showed the most emotion of all our children, so she approached his overreaction with caution, yearning to learn the entire truth.

"I don't know, but he's lost his mind."

I came into the house. Luke looked at me, let out some combination of a grunt and a squeal, and then ran upstairs.

"You're throwing balls at him?" Lorri laughed, expecting to get the full story from me.

"Yep," I affirmed. "Sure was."

She just looked at me.

Though I was hurling them at him to teach him a lesson, as I examine my motives, I was also doing it to improve his performance on the baseball field. In fact, this was my primary concern. Now, to clarify, it's not *always* bad to help your child improve his or her performance (especially if your child asks you for help), but when there is a greater emphasis on performance than there is on character, you are planting the seeds for a future identity crisis in your child. ✪

And, just like our stop in Spencer, my attention toward Luke's performances in the arena of sports eventually caused him to snap. When I took things to the extreme—whether it was chewing him out for three hours straight on a car ride or chucking T-balls at him—Luke took it personally. And now I understand why. He felt worthless.

Maybe Luke *did* need more discipline on the basketball court, but in

---

✪

LUKE: It's really interesting to go back and read these stories because it shows me how much Dad rewired his thinking since my junior high days. Through high school and college, I never felt any pressure at all from Dad to perform. I felt like he loved me for who I was, not what

I did. I think it should give parents a lot of hope, that, even if you elevate your child's performance too much, you can always change your ways like Dad did.

actuality, I was the one who needed more discipline as a parent. Maybe Luke *did* have a lot more to learn as a baseball player, but what he taught me was that I had a lot more to learn as a parent.

***

Another thing that Luke taught me, oddly around the same time we had the heart-to-heart talk in Spencer, was how to say "I love you." Looking back, I guess the prevalent theme in my mistakes as a parent seems to be that I had no idea how to show affection to my children through my words.

Remember the Christmas Eve when I was six years old and my dad grabbed my hand? Well, it remains such a vivid picture in my mind because my father didn't show affection very much. When he grabbed my hand, part of me was shocked; but it also felt exactly right. As I've said, it's the best Christmas gift I've ever received. I don't even remember what actual gift I got that year. I grew up knowing Dad loved me because of his actions; it was just never expressed verbally.

Similarly, I will always remember the day when I left the farmhouse and went off to college at Iowa State University. Dad shook my hand before I got in my car and drove off the farm. His handshake was strong and firm and confident, and he had a $20 bill in his palm. Another instance that showed Dad loved me.

When Luke, Tyler, and Cody were born, I went through parenting believing I could raise them like my father raised me: loving them through my actions. I never thought I would have to express it to them verbally because my dad didn't express it to me that way. It might sound silly, but saying "I love you" to my children never crossed my mind. Ever. It sounded weird, even—until Lorri pointed out that I was the one who sounded weird for *not* saying it.

When the boys were young, Lorri would often go into the boys' room and read them a bedtime story. She would get about three-quarters of the way through, set the book on the bed, tell them, "I love you," then leave the room. I would come in and finish the story;

then I would tuck them in, turn the lights off, and tell them, "Good night."

"I love you!" they would sometimes say.

I would pause, unsure how to respond.

"Okay!" I would say. "Thanks!"

And I would shut the door.

I think they eventually just stopped saying it to me because I never said it back.

Lorri and I had several conversations about it. I had never heard someone say "I love you" from a child to a parent or from a parent to a child. I wasn't sure what to do with it. I wasn't sure how to take it.

"Tell them you love them," she'd say.

"They *know* I love them," I'd tell her.

"But how do they know?" she'd ask.

"I knew my father loved me," I'd say.

There was an obvious difference in our upbringing and our backgrounds, and it really frustrated Lorri that I was being so stubborn about saying it to our children. But it felt so uncomfortable.

Slowly, Lorri helped me open up to the idea of being more affectionate. Several years later, I remember visiting Iowa, and Lorri challenged me to hug my mother. I did, and it felt like she melted in my arms—she wasn't used to her family showing much affection, either. But it was powerful.

Luke remembers being in junior high—around the same time we had our talk in Spencer—and attending a Bible study at church the day we attacked Afghanistan following September 11. Everyone was talking about being on the brink of war.

The conversation at Bible study, he says, evolved from war to losing loved ones. One of his friends said his biggest regret in life was never telling his father that he loved him before he passed. Hearing this story had a big impact on Luke.

He came home late that night, Lorri and I were in bed, and we heard him coming up the basement stairs. He opened our door.

"Hey Dad," he said. "Good night!"

He paused for a little. We could tell he had something on his mind.

"Uhhhh, I love you!" he said, and scurried out of our bedroom.

I found it weird at the time. I think Lorri was touched by it. ✿

CODY: "I found it weird."
Haha, a typical reaction from Dad.

It took a while before I actually said it back to Luke. I had my own way of telling him I loved him. We spent time together. We had a blast together. And, whereas Lorri might have been telling him "I love you" at night, he and I always did a little handshake.

But then he started saying "I love you" before he went off to bed each night, and I didn't know what to do. �֍

It seemed so unnatural, so forced. It was something I had *never* heard before. ✖

One weekend, Luke and I were serving communion together at a church retreat. Luke was in high school by this point. We had served communion to the congregation next to one another in church before, but that weekend we served communion *to* one another. There was something special about it, and I can't really explain it. That weekend was the first time Luke says that I hugged him. ✖

Soon after, I told him "I love you" for the first time. Now, I can't stop saying it to my children. Even as the boys went through high school, Lorri and I made sure to always go into their rooms at night and tell them that we loved them. Oftentimes, these end-of-the-day conversations were when they would open up to us the most.

Many times, parents stop hugging their teenagers or "tucking them in" because they are at "that age" where

LUKE: Dad would just grunt like a caveman.

LUKE: In high school, whenever I listened to country-artist Bucky Covington's song "A Father's Love," it made me think of Dad. Even if he wouldn't say "I love you," I knew he loved me because of the things he did for me. But still, I wondered why he just wouldn't say it.

LUKE: Between junior high and high school, I saw our handshake evolve to a pat on the back, and Dad's grunt (after I told him that I loved him) evolve to a "You too!" Not too long after communion, when he hugged me for the first time, he started saying "I love you" to me on a continual basis.

it's no longer "cool." But, in actuality, they are never too old or too cool for that. Your children are never too old for you to hug them and tell them that you love them.

⁂

Luke also taught me a lot in the aspect of faith. I was raised Catholic and Lorri was raised Lutheran, but we wanted to raise our children in the same sect of Christianity because we didn't want them to be pulled in two different directions. When we started having children, we always took our boys to the local Lutheran church in Washington. After Sunday service, we would come home and sometimes the boys would put on their own church service for Lorri and me. This happened most often when Luke was nine, Tyler was six, and Cody was three. Luke would pretend to preach a sermon; Tyler would play the only song he knew on the piano (it wasn't even a religious song); and Cody would play with toy cars or something. ❈ Lorri and I, of course, were in the congregation.

As Luke grew older, the Sunday sermons he gave to us when he was nine became thoughts and conversa-

CODY: Hey, those Hot Wheels cars were an important part of our church service!

tions between us about Jesus and faith. Luke taught me how important it is to have a *relationship* with God. Faith, to me, had always been very structured and based on tradition. Not that these things are bad—I appreciate my Catholic roots—but Luke helped me apply my faith and experience God on a day-to-day basis.

Luke had a relationship with God that was attractive to me. He prayed in a way that was attractive to me. Luke taught me that I didn't have to work so hard, that I didn't have to always be doing more and more to have a proper standing with the Lord. Because Luke had such a deep relationship with God, it helped me have a deeper relationship with God. And if your own son can teach you something as essential and foundational as saying "I love you" or following Jesus, I figure I should listen to him. So I did. And I keep listening.

✴

I often tell people that Luke blazed the trail for his two younger brothers—but he also carried me along with him. I really believe that I learned a lot from each of the boys, but especially from Luke because he was the oldest.

In each situation, it was humbling for me to take a step back and realize that I was wrong, or not entirely correct, and to remove myself from the situation and learn from my son. I realized that my status as a parent does not mean everything I did was right. The old Montgomery Gentry song "Back When I Knew It All" really resonated with me—though I thought I knew it all, I always seemed to be learning so much more.

This is one of the most important lessons I have earned as a parent: *My children can teach me how to be a better parent.* If I expected my children to learn from their mistakes, then I, as a parent, should also learn from my own mistakes. I learned the value in admitting I was wrong. This demonstrated strength, not weakness.

Of course, there was a time to discipline my kids, but when it came to Luke's performance in the realm of athletics, it was more important for me to lend a hand of support rather than put on my coaching cap. I learned that there were two simple, more encouraging phrases I could say to him in regard to athletics: "I'm proud of you" and "Have fun." Sports psychologist Jarrod Spencer, author of *The Sky Is Not the Limit,* says that athletes commonly rank the ride home with their parents as their worst sports memory. Spencer (his last name, ironically) suggests that it's one reason why seventy-five percent of kids stop playing sports by age thirteen. Proactive Coaching researchers suggest that it's vital for parents to adopt the phrase: "I love to watch you play."

I'll always remember the day my older brother approached me after a basketball game in high school and said, "You know what? I'm really proud of you." It meant so much to me for the sheer fact I always looked up to him and tried to emulate him in everything. And, though it meant a lot to me, I never thought of saying it to my very own children for some reason.

But something about our stop in Spencer made me realize that basketball should be fun, and therefore our car rides should be fun, and thus our talks on those car rides should be fun. My obsession with Luke's performance was robbing the entire experience of fun from Luke. I was becoming a "helicopter parent," constantly hovering. I was continually trying to control the situation, unsatisfied until I said everything I felt like I needed to say. But considering all the other hardships of life, sports, of all things, should be fun.

The following weekend, I was determined to change. I told myself, "I will say one positive thing after the game and will not say anything else about his performance unless he asks for my opinion." (Interestingly enough, my children always seemed to ask for my opinion once I learned to stop forcing it upon them.) I admit: It was hard.

On the way back to Washington on Sunday, I deeply wanted to talk about the tournament, as that was my habit, and I had gathered so many thoughts from the weekend in my head. I knew what he had done wrong; but I also tried to make a mental note of all the things he had done right. Still, I allowed Luke to direct the flow of our conversation.

"You know what would be cool, Dad?" he said to me.

"What's that?" I said.

"If we created a basketball camp."

"Oh, really?" I queried.

"Yeah," he said, "we could buy some land, put up a farmhouse, build a basketball court, and also have animals on the property."

I noticed that his eyes were lighting up.

"I like it," I told him.

His imagination started to run free, and he began talking more and more excitedly about this hypothetical basketball camp.

"We could wake up the campers early in the morning to go milk the cows, and then they could come into the farmhouse and have breakfast!" he said, talking faster and faster. "Then, once their work on the farm is done, they can go to the gym! We could do drills, and then in the afternoon, they could clean out the cattle stalls and different things. After that, they could scrimmage in the evening." 🏀

LUKE: It's crazy to go back and think about this.

"I love that idea," I told him. "We teach them basketball but also teach them character on the farm."

"Yes, *exactly,*" Luke said. And he went on and on and on.

That particular Sunday, Luke was the one talking to me the entire car ride.

Every lengthy car ride, our conversations always seemed to end up back at his idea for a basketball camp on a farm. He would add more details to the camp experience each time and explain the purpose of specific tasks on the farm and basketball drills on the court. He had practically built this entire concept in his mind, and it continued to grow and evolve with each car ride.

When Tyler played AAU, I had the same mindset with him on our long car rides: *Tell him one positive thing, and never say anything else about his performance unless he asks for my opinion.*

Though Luke would talk about a basketball camp, Tyler and I didn't talk about basketball at all. Instead, we would invent things together. His coolest invention (which should have made the Zeller family millions, by the way) was a helicopter that attached to a car. What made the "Helicar" unique was that, if it was in "attachment mode," you could crawl through the hood of the car to the cockpit of the helicopter, thus allowing a single person to operate it. I can still remember some of the meticulous details of his inventions because Tyler would spend hours upon hours mapping them out—down to every last nut and bolt.

Once, I remember pulling into our driveway in Washington and walking into our house. Lorri was working in the kitchen.

"How was your weekend?" she

CODY: I remember that Tyler was obsessed with the idea of pushing a button and something happening. He would always say, "What if you pushed a button and *this* happened? What if you pushed a button, and *that* happened?"

asked Tyler.

"It was great!" Tyler exclaimed. "We invented a helicopter-car."

Then he proceeded to give Lorri a brief, forty-five-minute synopsis of our invention and why everyone in America should have one. ✸

Our inventions, in fact, may have been the only thing that made Tyler talk in depth about *anything*. He would spend hours building things alone in his room, and we would of-

TYLER: That thing was awesome.

ten have to force him to come out and socialize. Lorri and I always joked that Tyler could probably stare at a spoon for an hour—just studying it. By the end of the hour, he could tell you what he was going to do with the spoon, how it was designed, and why it was designed the way it was. He would just stare at stuff, and Lorri and I both knew to leave him alone. ✸

Lorri would politely nod as Tyler explained our engineering epiphanies, but once Tyler would go upstairs, she would ask me, "Did you guys really talk about that the entire trip back?"

TYLER: I *would* take offense to all of this, but it's all true.

"Yep," I would say.

"You guys are so weird," she'd respond. "Was there even a basketball tournament this weekend, or did you guys go to an engineering convention?"

Sometimes, Cody and I would talk about sports or listen to ESPN radio. But mostly, he would either crack jokes or sleep. Looking back, it's weird to think that my conversations with Cody, of all people, were the most normal. ✸

CODY: I'm the weird one? Thanks, Dad.

Overall, combatting my desire to control each and every situation on the basketball floor and demand athletic perfection from my children taught me a lot about parenting in general: Allow your children to go through the process, whatever it may be.

It's hard to see your child make a mistake that you *know* is the wrong decision, but you have to let them make mistakes if you want them to grow by going through the process. God does the same thing with us. He extends free will to us so we can choose to follow Him. Sometimes, not following Him leads to severe earthly consequences, but this is our choice. A loving God would not force His children to do anything. And He doesn't. He gives us the choice to follow Him.

The tendency as a parent is to tell your children *everything* to prevent them from making a mistake, but all this does is exhaust your children. And truthfully, so much control is exhausting for a parent, too. So what is the point of exhausting everyone and creating unnecessary conflict in your home?

The important thing is that your children learn from their mistakes; it's unrealistic to think they'll never make mistakes. God does not expect us to be perfect—He expects His grace to change us. How can we, as parents, expect our children to be perfect?

A lot of times, I wanted Luke to go down a certain trail, but instead, he would venture down a different trail. My tendency was to try to force him down the trail I wanted him to go. But, at the end of the day, especially as he entered his teenage years and got into high school, I had to recognize that it was his life to live. All I could do was give him a foundation for him to base his decisions. Even if he went down a different trail, I hoped the foundation we raised him on would be enough to guide his decision-making on whatever trail it was that he chose.

This mindset of surrender was ultimately freeing—scary, but freeing. I realized that it wasn't all up to me. It was important for me to lead my children the right way and guide them the right way but not *force* each and every step. Instead I eventually saw the enjoyment in watching them go through each process, growing through each process, and even helping them through the process if they wanted my help. Usually, they did. My children trusted me more once I stopped trying to control them.

What amazes me most is that God redeemed the car rides that used to be torturous for Luke. God took one of my most embarrassing, humbling moments as a parent—when I could tangibly see the pain my attitude and actions had caused—and He made something beautiful out of it.

The idea that was birthed on our four-hour trips from Fort Wayne to Washington stuck with him throughout high school and college. A local television station once interviewed Luke in high school and asked him what he wanted to do when he got older. He didn't say he wanted to play in the NBA, though these were the expectations placed on him across the state of Indiana; instead, he told them he wanted to start a basketball camp. In college at Notre Dame, he gave a presentation for one of his capstone entrepreneurship classes about one of his business ideas—a character-building basketball camp. And a couple years later, he actually started it. A decade after our infamous car ride, Luke's hypothetical basketball camp became a reality, and DistinXion was born.

DistinXion hosts camps across the state of Indiana and uses basketball and cheerleading as an avenue to teach character to children—not quite the farm he envisioned on our car rides, but it ultimately serves the exact same purpose. I have a feeling the kids are happy they don't have to milk cows, anyway.

On the first day of camp, when parents are invited to stay for the first few hours, I usually tell the story about stopping in Spencer and being humbled by Luke's question, "Was there anything I did right?" One time, a father approached me after my talk.

"I didn't like that story you told," the father told me.

"Why is that?" I asked.

"Because you were describing me," he said. He paused. "Thank you."

Most ironically, I find it comical that the story I always tell to parents is at the very camp my son dreamt up, once I finally swallowed my pride and learned to shut my own mouth. I'm continually amazed by what God can make of my mistakes if I am willing to admit they are mistakes. God made something beautiful of it all.

Unfortunately, we haven't seen any fruition from Tyler's ideas yet. I'm still waiting for someone to manufacture the Helicar.

WRECKS AND RECKLESSNESS
by Lorri Zeller

Some people have the misconception that our children were perfect, little—er, big—angels in high school. I think they get this idea not just from their basketball accolades but also from their success in the classroom. Luke finished high school with a 4.0 GPA and was a co-valedictorian, Tyler had a 3.97 GPA and was No. 3 in his class, and Cody had a 3.99 GPA and was named salutatorian.

Tyler actually intentionally aimed for third place (and got it) because he didn't want to give a speech at graduation. A couple A-minuses in his freshman English class took care of that. The rest of his grades were straight A's. Cody tried to do the same thing but the top two students *tied* and were named co-valedictorians, thus pushing Cody up to second. He was so mad! And yes, he gave a speech.

Like many of these stories, each situation fits their personalities quite well. Luke is a big goal-setter and achiever, Tyler is quiet and didn't like public speaking, and Cody is, well, Cody—his plan just backfired.

And, though we are very proud of our children's accomplishments on the basketball floor and in the classroom, they were *far* from perfect in high school. Their high school years were their first taste of freedom, and they didn't always handle this freedom maturely.

꧁꧂

As Steve learned with Luke, you can't expect your children to be perfect. You have to let them learn on their own. You must let them go through the process.

This, however, becomes much more difficult to simply write off as a "process" as your children grow older. Why? Well, the problems, or potential problems, seem to be on a much larger scale than simply failing to box out on a basketball court. As a child's responsibilities increase, as he or she ventures further and further into the world, the problems also have the potential to be more severe. At sixteen years old, a child may be able to drive a car, but this also means he has the potential to wreck the car. At twenty-one years old, one may be able to drink alcohol, but this also means he has the potential to abuse the privilege, which often leads to worse decisions. More responsibility *can* lead to more reckless decisions.

The paradox is that this makes you want to control them more, and yet, if you try to control them more, they may lash out and make even worse decisions if they feel like they are being micromanaged. We learned to trust in our own parenting—that we had equipped them to decipher what is right or wrong, helpful or harmful. Not that disciplining your children is non-existent as they grow older, because there is certainly a time for it, but eventually, parenting must move toward trust. And with trust also comes grace.

⁂

One day I woke up, and Luke was six foot ten and a junior in high school—I couldn't believe how fast time had flown. It seemed like just yesterday Steve was throwing T-balls at him in the backyard and he was running inside crying to me. He was no longer our little boy. Our firstborn son was a grown man and much more grown than we ever had imagined. Now that same little boy, who was always excitedly talking about an imaginary basketball camp, could drive a car, have a girlfriend, and make decisions on his own. It all happened in the blink of an eye.

Luke was developing into an incredible leader, too. We could always tell that he had leadership qualities; Steve often calls him the "trailblazer" for both Tyler and Cody. But these qualities really developed in high school.

His freshman year, for example, a group of seniors on the team wondered if they could fit a seven-footer into a trashcan—so they performed the experiment on Luke during passing period. ✸

It wasn't malicious hazing. They were just being boys. Times were different back then. But he lost his wallet in the process, and he certainly didn't like being the punch line of a joke. Luckily, a night janitor found his wallet and returned it to him the following day.

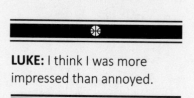

LUKE: I think I was more impressed than annoyed.

When he came home from school that night, however, he asked Steve how he should handle it if it were to happen again. Luke has always been pretty sensitive, and he *hated* getting in trouble, so he didn't want a teacher to get mad at him if he stood up for himself and ignited some commotion in the hallway. But he also wanted to make sure the "stuff a seven-footer in the trash can" incident was only a one-time thing.

"You've got to stand up for yourself," Steve told him. "I can't go stand up for you anymore. And depending how far they push it is how far you can push it."

"What if I get in trouble?" Luke asked Steve.

"There are certain things that are okay to get in trouble over," Steve told him. "If you're standing up for something you know is right, something you believe in, getting in trouble is not all that bad. That's the way I was taught."

This is what high school became for all of our boys in regard to our parenting—giving them the freedom to approach us for advice instead of overwhelming them with it.

The following week, they tried to do it again, but he stood up to them. "You did it once," he told them. "Now it's over. Done." He came home that evening and was excited to explain it all to us. They didn't mess with him again. ✸

Both Luke's faith and his personality really took on a new identity in high school. Of course, we had always taken the boys to church, but in high school, Luke really began to

CODY: I think if my teammates had tried to do this to me when I was a freshman, I would have just

gotten in the trashcan myself. If someone is trying to play a joke on me, then I want to be a part of it.

make his faith his own, so much, in fact, that it was inspiring to Steve and me. It can be a beneficial thing when you give your children space throughout their adolescent years to figure things out and ask some of life's biggest questions for the first time. He had a desire to grow in knowledge and wisdom, and he did this in community with others but also on his own. His Christian faith was quickly becoming the centerpiece of his life and the core to his entire existence. Steve and I called ourselves "Christians," but there was something that was truly inspiring and different about Luke's pursuit of God. His faith encompassed his entire life.

His passion carried over from God to people, too. It soon became apparent that Luke was a people-person and a caregiver. He talked to *everyone*. And if someone needed something, he was there. This sometimes got him in trouble because he would say "yes" to too many things and overbook himself. If he had to say "no" or couldn't help, he would feel guilty. Regardless, Steve and I were both proud of him for the kind of heart he had and encouraged by the type of faith he displayed.

At the end of the day, however, he was also a high school kid—and high school kids can do some stupid things. Luke did some really stupid things. �

The worst occurred on the road. He treated his driver's license more like a NASCAR contract. He sometimes seemed to think his 2001 shark blue Dodge Avenger was a Ferrari.

LUKE: Gah! I knew the compliments would end eventually!

One day, for whatever reason, he decided it'd be a good idea to drag race one of his teammates down Sugarland Road—a straightaway near our house. He had another one of his teammates in the car with him. Apparently, all of our children drove fast down this road. Of course, they didn't admit this to us until several years later.

During the "race," however, Luke came over a hill and got airborne. Only the Lord knows how fast he was going. ✴

TYLER: He was going 120 miles per hour.

LUKE: Not saying anything.

Luke panicked, since he was flying through the air and all, and he slammed on his brakes as soon as his wheels hit the ground again. The result was a fifty-foot skid mark and a screech that probably made people in the area think missiles were being fired at Washington, Indiana.

His car was fine. He was fine. And no harm was done. He actually drove his car back to school and went to class.

Later in the afternoon, Washington High School principal Gary Puckett came into the athletic office, where I worked as a secretary for a number of years, and started talking to me.

"I just got a phone call from a man who lives on Sugarland Road," Mr. Puckett said. "He said he saw a car going at least ninety miles per hour before it slammed on its brakes. He gave me the license plate number, and your son Luke's car is the vehicle that came up in our system."

I immediately defended Luke.

"I don't think Luke would do that," I said.

Luke's high school coach, Dave Omer, could also hear our conversation, and he jumped to Luke's defense, as well.

"Luke doesn't drive like that," Coach Omer said. "Someone must have been driving his car."

"All right," Mr. Puckett said, "let's get Luke in here and figure out who was driving his car."

Mr. Puckett made a couple of phone calls, and Luke entered the athletic office soon after. Luke sat down casually, slouching in his chair, and tried to act cool and relaxed.

Mr. Puckett explained the situation to Luke. "Who took your car and did this?" Mr. Puckett eventually asked.

"Well," Luke said, "I was actually the one that made the skid marks."

There was a pause.

"That was *you?!*" I exclaimed.

Luke nodded.

I was mad at him and embarrassed. I had defended him to both his principal and basketball coach. I never imagined he would do such a thing.

After school, I drove the same way and saw the skid marks stretching from one block of the street to the next block. I started crying. I went from being embarrassed to scared. It was easy to tell from the skid marks that he was going way too fast.

If he had wrecked, it could have been fatal.

As the evening ensued, I transitioned from sadness to anger. I wanted to take his keys away until he was forty. I couldn't understand how someone could be so irresponsible and careless as to put his entire life at risk. I was fuming.

Drag-racing down a county road? Seriously?

I felt like there were two worlds colliding. On one hand was the man Luke was becoming—a man of faith, a man with a gigantic heart, a man who was beginning to bring "the Zeller name" tremendous honor. On the other hand was an irresponsible child who had nearly killed himself (and/or his teammate) over, to put it bluntly, one of the most reckless things I could possibly fathom.

Luckily, Steve got home from work and was there to calm me down. The last time I was *that* mad was probably when Tyler forgot about baseball practice, then forgot his baseball mitt, then didn't listen to a word I said all the way home. This, however, seemed to take my anger to an entirely different level because of the reality that Luke could have been seriously hurt or killed. What if his wheels would have moved a *smidgen* once he landed? Going eighty or ninety miles per hour? ✴

Whatever speed it was they were traveling, he could have flipped the car—several times. Luke is lucky his little stunt didn't kill him or someone else. But he's even luckier that I didn't kill him. ✴

When Luke returned home after basketball practice, we waited for him to say something to us. But we

> ✴
>
> **TYLER:** Mom always thinks I am exaggerating, but I'm not. Luke *told* me he was going 120 miles per hour.
>
> **LUKE:** Not saying anything.

could tell when he walked in the door by his pale complexion that he was absolutely petrified. It was obvious the severity of the situation

════════════════════════════

⇐ ✳

LUKE: Now, that's the truth.

════════════════════════════

had weighed on him throughout the day. He was quiet and wouldn't make eye contact with us.

"I did something stupid today," he said.

"I know," Steve said. (I kept my mouth shut. I knew if I opened it, I would go off.)

Luke shook his head in disbelief.

"I just—I just don't know why I did that," Luke said sincerely, obviously shaken. He looked at Steve, expecting to be sentenced to his room for life.

"You made a mistake," Steve shrugged. "We understand."

Luke still didn't make eye contact with us.

"Thank God you didn't get hurt," Steve said compassionately.

Luke nodded, looking down at the floor.

"You can't let it happen again," Steve said.

"I won't," Luke said.

"It was just one mistake. But you have to take responsibility for your actions."

Steve made Luke apologize to the parents of the teammate who was riding with him, but that was it. He decided no punishment was necessary. The experience was traumatic enough on its own. I wanted to punish him, probably primarily out of my own fear of losing him. A deserving or "fair" punishment after something so reckless might have been taking away his car. After all, he didn't deserve the privilege of driving a car. But instead, grace was extended.

〰〰

Steve always tells a story about growing up, when he and his siblings were doing their daily chores. His brother, Ted, was on the rototiller making rows to plant in the garden. When his mom wasn't looking, Steve and his brother Joel would throw dirt clods at Ted. His mother became upset because the rows weren't straight, and Ted became upset because she didn't notice Steve and Joel tossing the dirt clods at him, thus causing him to make wobbly rows.

After Steve's mom snapped at Ted several times about the rows, he hit his breaking point. "Mom!" he exclaimed. "You're a bitch!"

And at that precise moment, the rototiller died, and everyone heard him. The kids believed Ted might die that evening, too. As goes the country song "Choices" by George Jones, sometimes we live and die by the choices we make.

Steve says that time suddenly froze. Ted was incredibly embarrassed and ashamed. His face reddened, and he lowered his head. He knew he would be punished. "Punished," actually, was probably an understatement.

Later that evening, the kids were playing baseball out by the barn when Steve's father returned from the fields and approached them.

"Ted, did you have a problem with your mother today?" Steve's father said.

"Yeah," Ted said sheepishly.

Ted went on to explain what had happened, that he had been angry, continued to get more angry the more his mother didn't notice Steve and Joel throwing dirt clods at him, and eventually snapped right when the rototiller died.

To the dismay of all the children, Steve's father threw back his head in disbelief and laughed, "So you're telling me that you called your mother a bitch, and right at that moment, the rototiller died and she heard you?"

Ted nodded.

Steve's father laughed again. All the children looked at one another, confused.

"Don't you think it was disrespectful to call your mother that word whether she heard you or not?" his father added.

Ted nodded again. He was utterly ashamed.

"It doesn't matter that she heard you," his dad continued. "What matters is that you said it. Do you understand?"

"Yes sir," Ted said.

"All right," Steve's dad said, picking up a baseball mitt and tossing it to him. "Let's play some baseball."

The children all looked at one another, shocked. Was Ted, or anyone for that matter, going to get in any trouble at all? His father turned around as he walked out into the yard and addressed the children.

"If any of you *ever* disrespect your mother like that again, you'll never see the light of day," his father threatened. He paused. "What're you guys looking at? Let's play baseball."

Ted never got spanked. He never got punished. But he never called his mother anything ever again, and he did a much better job respecting her from that point forward because of the grace his father extended to him.

Extending grace isn't always the solution, but if it's used sparingly in appropriate situations, the effects *can* be long lasting. Forty years later, after all, Steve still remembers that entire incident. If anything, the situation probably heightened their respect for their parents. If that kind of disrespect were displayed ever again, after all, the consequences would be *really* severe.

Luke also knew that if he ever pulled a stunt like he did in his car again, he probably wouldn't have a social life. For Luke's sake, I suppose it's a good thing Steve remembers what took place with his father and Ted—or else he still might not have his license today.

⁂

The most ridiculous thing about Luke's high-speed incident is that it happened again with one of our other children. You'd hope an incident that was nearly as catastrophic as Luke's would be a wake-up call, not only to Luke but also to everyone close to him like, ahem, his brothers, but apparently, it wasn't. ✺

One day around Thanksgiving, when Tyler was a junior, Cody was sick so he stayed home from school. Cody had a math test that afternoon, however, so when Tyler came home for lunch (all the students at Washington were given a forty-

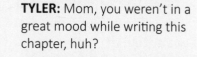

TYLER: Mom, you weren't in a great mood while writing this chapter, huh?

minute lunch break each day), Cody decided to ride back with Tyler to take his test at school. I saw them briefly, as I had also returned home for lunch, but then I drove back to the athletic office for work.

As they were heading back to school, traveling down the same hilly straightaway where Luke thought he'd act like he was in *The Fast and the Furious,* Tyler was also driving way too fast. As the straightaway came to an end and they approached the coming left-turn, Tyler tried to slow down and lost control of the vehicle.

What happened next is nothing short of miraculous. His car flew off the right side of the road, where there was a light pole and a cement culvert square. Basically, with no time to dodge either, the car still traveling at a ridiculous speed, he had a choice: Would he choose to ram into the light pole or the culvert?

He chose to do neither, attempting to whip the car back onto the road, though there was no time to do so, and he ended up ramming into the culvert square on the passenger side.

Considering he had just rammed his car into a gigantic cement block, the culvert should have stopped the car violently. However, Tyler must have hit the culvert at just the right angle because instead of stopping the car, the car broke through the cement, clipping a chunk off the culvert, and the car ramped into the air. The car landed with a *crunch* on all four wheels, where it came to a miraculous stop in the center of the road. Tyler was fine. Cody was fine. The car was totaled.

Tyler gave me a call on his cell phone.

"I just wrecked the car," he told me, emotionless.

"What?" I said, shocked because I had seen them literally minutes before. "You just left the house!" I said.

"I know," Tyler said. "I crashed by the Smiths' house." (The Smiths were a family in Washington that had a son who graduated with Luke. They lived less than a mile from us.)

"All right," I sighed, "be there in a second."

A minute later I arrived at the scene. The car was absolutely destroyed, much worse than I had pictured in my head when Tyler had calmly told me he had wrecked. Tyler probably wouldn't have had a hint of panic in his tone even if his car had exploded to a thousand pieces.

"Oh, my gosh!" I panicked, looking at both Tyler and Cody.

"Mom, it's fine," Tyler said. In typical Tyler fashion, he was expressionless and did not want any drama.

I couldn't stop looking at the car. The entire left side looked like a boulder had fallen on it. The bottom of the car was obliterated from their landing. The car was no longer drivable. I bombarded Tyler and Cody with questions, trying to figure out exactly what happened. I think they were trying to figure it out, too. To this day, it's still hard to logically explain how the car ended up in the place that it did.

"So why is the windshield cracked?" I eventually said, noticing a large crack in the middle of the window beneath the rearview mirror.

"Oh, that's from Cody's head," Tyler said nonchalantly.

My mind started racing. *How did his head hit the windshield? And if it was from Cody's head, why was the crack in the middle of the windshield, not on the passenger's side?*

"Cody's head?!" I exclaimed. "Were you not wearing a seatbelt?!"

"No," Cody said, "I was putting my shoes on."

It suddenly dawned on me that if the cement block had stopped Tyler's car in its tracks like it logically should have, Cody would have gone flying out the front windshield. I buried my head in my hands. I wanted to strangle Tyler for driving so fast, strangle Cody for not wearing a seatbelt, strangle Tyler again for driving too fast knowing his brother hadn't fastened his seatbelt, but at the same time hold onto them for all of eternity, never letting go. I couldn't believe how lucky they were. It was truly a miracle. And it wasn't the first windshield Cody had broken with his head. �

A couple of neighbors had come out to help, and a boy in Cody's grade had also pulled up with his truck. "You want a ride to school?" he asked Cody.

"Sure," Cody said, hopping in the car, "might as well."

In all reality, Cody shouldn't have even been walking, yet here he was going to school to take a test. ✱

He still prides himself on acing his math test that day despite what

---

CODY: Each time Tyler tells this story in front of a group of people, it gets more and more dramatic. The truth is that I popped up and hit my head on the windshield, and my butt landed on the center console. Tyler bumped me back into my seat with his arm. Last time Tyler told the story, he said that he grabbed me and pushed me back into my seat. Give it another five years, and Tyler will be telling people how he grabbed my shoelace as I was flying out the window and pulled me back into the car.

CODY: Nothing is more important than earning an education!!!

---

had happened moments before and the gigantic bump on his head.

Tyler and Cody made it to basketball practice that evening, too. I had something going on at church that night, so they had to call their father for a ride home once practice was over. The fact that they had to call him for a ride was probably the same humbling, humiliating feeling Steve's brothers and sisters felt when they had to admit their wrongdoing at the dinner table. I wanted Steve to deal with them anyway. I was still processing it all. I was furious over their poor decision-making, especially Tyler's, but I also felt fortunate they could walk, not to mention go to basketball practice. ❊

TYLER: That night, I remember walking out of the gymnasium with Cody.

CODY: Dad was standing next to his truck with his arms crossed, wearing his big, old winter jacket. "This isn't going to be good," I said to Tyler.

We started walking as slow as we possibly could, trying not to make eye contact with Dad.

"Well," Dad said in his low voice, "there's two lucky guys."

TYLER: We knew we were doomed.

Not always, but sometimes, grace has the potential to demonstrate trust and be more of a powerful tool than discipline. Steve once again extended grace to Tyler and Cody after their accident, just as he had with Luke. And we believe it motivated them to make better decisions because we trusted them that they had learned their lesson.

After Tyler's accident, I remember Steve telling me, "I hope we got a two-for-one scare with both Tyler and Cody." And I believe that is the effect it had. Tyler realized how quickly his future could have changed. And when Cody was going through driver's education two years later, his instructor says that he was only going thirty-five miles per hour on the interstate.

"Uhhhh," his instructor said, "you can go a little faster than this."

Cody finally got the car up to fifty miles per hour. ✳

Now, we disciplined our boys in high school, too, but in these situations, we decided to extend grace. The point of both discipline and grace is to move your children toward change. If Luke would have kept racing with his friends, if Tyler would have kept driving fast, and if Cody would have made the *same* mistake he saw *both* of his brothers make, then we would have had no choice but to resort to punishment. ✳

CODY: I swear this never happened.

TYLER: No one drives slower than Cody.

LUKE: Cody is the slowest driver ever.

Steve would often tell them, "Don't make the same mistake twice." Sometimes, one mistake is all it takes for your life to drastically change. That's why we felt like each experience was traumatic enough to teach them valuable lessons. It's not always about punishing them; rather, it's about empowering them.

CODY: I didn't have time to make the same mistakes they did. I was too busy breaking their records on the basketball floor.

It's also important to remember that they were older when these things happened. At that age, we felt we could reason with them a little more while still being a parent. When they are five years old, if you keep extending grace to them, they will think forgiveness without consequences is the norm. In high school, however, we found it more powerful if we trusted them to make right decisions rather than inject fear into them for making wrong decisions.

And, in each situation, despite how livid we were, we felt grace had a greater ability to empower them in their lives and decision-making moving forward. ✳

This must be the underlying factor behind principles you imple-

LUKE: I'm glad Mom brought this up, because I think this is the way biblical grace acts, as well. Grace, to me, is probably the word that best describes Christianity. It is the heart of the gospel. God's love, mercy, and grace are prevalent throughout the entire Bible, but it is in the ministry, death, and resurrection of Jesus Christ that grace is most magnificently demonstrated.

He died to forgive us of our sins and to stamp a new identity upon us. Through Christ, God forgives the sins of the world—past, present, and future. But grace that does not change us is not grace in its truest sense.

It's why the apostle Paul poses these questions in response to grace in Romans 6:1: "What shall we say, then? Shall we go on sinning so that grace may increase?"

He answers his own question in the following verses, Romans 6:2-4: *"By no means! We are those who have died to sin; how can we live in it any longer? Or don't you know that all of us who were baptized into Christ Jesus were baptized into his death? We were therefore buried with him through baptism into death in order that, just as Christ was raised from the dead through the glory of the Father, we too may live a new life."*

---

ment with your children (whether it's discipline, trust, grace, etc.)—to bring them into new life, to change them, to show them a better way to live than the way they are living, just like the grace that is talked about in the New Testament.

Help them experience life to the fullest.

〰️

Parents should give themselves some grace, too. We had to learn not to take the decisions our children made too personally. Did we raise Luke better than his decision to race down a straightaway with his friends? Gosh, I'd sure hope so. Did we raise Tyler better than driving recklessly with another human being in the passenger seat? Again, I'd sure hope so. But, just as God isn't surprised by our sin, don't be surprised by the irresponsible things your children might do. Both practically and spiritually, problems are normal, but they must also be dealt with. Problems are a part of growing up. Your response to these problems, however, determines how you can lead your children toward change.

As a parent, you must decide what route to take when problems arise. Some parents might think to themselves, "I'm mad, and I'm going to tell my children why I'm mad." This is what I naturally felt like doing after I found out about both of the boys' car accidents. But it is much more important for parents to make their children think about the impact their reckless decisions could have had rather than for parents to express their anger or displeasure. For example, though we didn't punish Luke or Tyler, we made Luke apologize to the parents of the teammate who was in the car with him, and we made sure that Tyler understood how he had put his younger brother's life in jeopardy. There are a number of ways to get your point across, and it's important to carefully evaluate which route will be most effective for your children. Parenting is not a cookie-cutter ordeal. There is no particular mold.

As mentioned at the beginning of the chapter, sometimes people make the wrong assumption that, just because we had three children who played in the NBA, excelled in school, and seemingly have squeaky-clean reputations, we therefore must be perfect parents and they must be perfect children. But, as you can see, that couldn't be further from the truth.

Kids will fail. The important thing is that they learn *when* they fail. We felt fortunate—blessed—that our children's failures didn't end tragically, especially when the decisions made were foolish enough that they could have.

Take problems seriously, but don't be surprised by them. Don't allow your mind to venture down the road that, just because your child did (fill in the blank), then you therefore must be a bad parent. Problems are a part of growing up. But implement strategies that will lead them toward *change*.

When the boys started excelling at basketball, people assumed we had moved to Washington because of its rich basketball history. When we moved from Minnesota to Indiana for Steve's job, however, Cody was six months old, Tyler was three, and Luke was six. We had no idea they would play basketball or even *like* basketball, for that matter. Growing up, they were just boys who enjoyed swimming in the hotel pool on vacation.

And yet, as Luke grew older, and kept growing and growing and growing, quickly gaining attention for his potential on the hardwood, it became apparent that God had His hand in bringing us to Washington, Indiana. Not only did God make Luke almost seven feet tall and give him a passion for basketball, but He also brought us to Indiana, where basketball is a religion, and specifically to Washington, where its basketball history is supreme.

Still, we couldn't have fathomed what was in store . . .

☙

Blazing the Trail

If you don't believe basketball is a religion in Indiana, one needs to look no further than Washington High School's famed gymnasium, the "Hatchet House," which seats 7,090 people—in a town with a population of about 12,000. It's the centerpiece of the town, its sanctuary. Basketball is Washington's heartbeat.

The Hatchet House is the twelfth largest high school gym in the country, but Washington is by far the smallest city on that list. Twelve of the fifteen largest gyms in the country are from Indiana. Built in 1967, it is the host of a Sectional and Regional almost every year, and is famous, not only for its size, but also for being the site of Richard Nixon's opening speech in his campaign for presidency in February 1968. Random, I know. The original Hatchet House, constructed in 1925, still stands next door as a junior high facility.

The gym, though large, is not grandiose in a showy sense. It is a symbol of Hoosier purity—its wooden bleachers representing simplicity, its cement structure a bulwark of unchanging values, its intimidating stadium seating illustrating the passion, focus, and support of an entire community, and the banners hanging in the rafters beneath the arch of its ceiling showing how all of these "old school" virtues can produce seven State championships. The Hatchet House represents everything Washington stands for and everything Indiana is.

The Washington High School Hatchets won a State championship in 1930, when their star center, Dave DeJernett, was the first African-American to start on a State championship team; they won two more State titles in 1941 and 1942 with an Indiana All-Star named Charlie Harmon, later the first African-American to play for the Cincinnati Reds.

Before Luke entered high school, however, the last time they had shown any sign of statewide basketball prominence was in the early 1980s under the leadership of Craig Neal, an Indiana All-Star who went on to play for Bobby Cremins at Georgia Tech, then was drafted by the Portland Trailblazers in 1988. Neal—nicknamed "Noodles"—was an assistant coach under Indiana University legend Steve Alford at both the University of Iowa and the University of New Mexico. He accepted the New Mexico head coaching role when his boyhood friend Alford took the UCLA head coaching job in 2013.

The Hatchets also had some stellar years in the late '70s under 1979 Indiana Mr. Basketball Steve Bouchie. He accumulated 1,311 career points and 842 career rebounds and helped lead them to three Sectional championships. He went on to win a national championship with the Indiana Hoosiers in 1981. He was drafted in the fourth round of the 1983 NBA Draft before playing overseas and entering the agricultural business soon after. In 2009, he was inducted into the Indiana Basketball Hall of Fame.

Most people in Washington talked about the "Craig Neal Days" and the "Steve Bouchie Days"—let alone those ancient State championships—as if they were long, lost forgotten memories. They were times that once were—the Neal and Bouchie eras the closest thing to basketball success in Washington since World War II. It seemed to be such a distant idea—real success, that is—and was discussed much more in the preservation of the past rather than the anticipation of the future. ✹

In a town that was as passionate about its basketball as Washington, a twenty-plus-year drought didn't settle well with fans. When Luke got to high school, they were a good team, just not a great team. They had finished 14-7 Luke's freshman

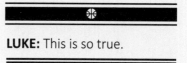

LUKE: This is so true.

season in 2002, 18-4 in 2003, and 18-5 in 2004; Luke averaged 15.3 points and 8.0 rebounds per game, 18.1 points and 8.3 rebounds per game, and 19.8 points and 9.4 rebounds, respectively. That all sounds pretty good, but here's the thing: They hadn't won a Sectional since 1983. In Indiana, a team must get past the Sectional, the first round of tournament play, then the Regional and Semi-State stages to have a chance at winning a State title. Heading into 2005, it had been twenty-two long years since the Hatchets had tasted any kind of postseason success, even at the Sectional stage.

One day, Craig Neal, who was coaching under Steve Alford at Iowa at the time, gave the Washington athletic office a call, where Lorri was working. Washington was trying to decide at the time what shoes the basketball team was going to wear—Reebok or Adidas—and Neal was supposedly going to help Washington get an Adidas deal because of his connections. Lorri picked up the phone when he called, though I'm not sure if he realized he was talking to the mother of Luke Zeller.

Lorri asked him about the possibility of the team's wearing Adidas shoes that year.

"Well," Lorri remembers him saying, "Adidas doesn't really know if they're interested because you guys haven't won a Sectional in twenty-two years [when he was a player], and Luke Zeller hasn't really done anything yet."

Lorri came home that night, and she was fuming. She told Washington head basketball coach Dave Omer about the situation, and he responded by saying, "That's fine; he can say whatever he wants. We'll just have to win a Sectional this year. And we'll do it while wearing Reebok shoes."

Two years before, it had actually appeared that ten-year head coach and future Indiana Basketball Hall of Famer Dave Omer's time with the Hatchets was coming to an end. Washington negotiated contracts in three-year terms, and his latest had ended after Luke's freshman season. They were debating whether or not they should renew his contract. Luke, however, really liked Coach Omer and he wanted him to stay at Washington. ✳

Luke wrote a letter to the school board, suggesting they renew Coach Omer's contract. He closed the letter with these words:

In all, I would like for Coach Omer to get his three-year contract. He has had to struggle through some tough times and now has the foundation built. Coach Omer should be given a chance to finish building a successful Washington basketball program.

Thank you for your time.

Sincerely,

Luke Zeller #40

LUKE: I always felt like Coach Omer and former Purdue University head coach Gene Keady could have been twins because of their style of coaching. No ear piercings, no long hair, etc. He ran a tight ship. I appreciated that style. I also thought Coach Omer was super passionate, intelligent, and I really felt like, under his direction, our team was on the brink of a breakthrough.

I am not sure if his letter had anything to do with it, but they ended up renewing his contract for three more years. He would get to coach Luke the remainder of his high school career and would have the opportunity to "finish building a successful Washington basketball program."

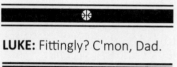

The story starts long before the 2005 season began—eleven years before on Luke's first day of first grade.

Luke was fittingly terrified that morning to leave us and get on the bus. ✷

He didn't know what to expect.

The bus eventually arrived; the door opened; and the driver looked down at a hesitant little boy, clenching his mother's hand, and looking up at the stairs fearfully, like it was a mountain to climb. The driver smiled at him and proceeded to walk down the steps of the bus and hold out her hand for Luke to take. He hesitantly let go of Lorri's hand, took the bus driver's hand, and walked with her up the stairs of the bus, looking over his shoulder apprehensively back at us.

LUKE: Fittingly? C'mon, Dad.

Lorri probably cried. I suppose it was cute. I just wanted him to man up. It was only a school bus. ✷

The bus driver's name was Wilda Omer, and she was the kindest woman you could ever meet. Over the next two years, this became her and Luke's tradition. She would take his hand and walk him up the stairs to his seat each time she picked him up.

TYLER: It was only a school bus, Luke.

As time passed, we learned that Washington's basketball coach, Dave Omer, was the husband of Wilda. Spend enough time in Washington, and you learn that everyone is either related or connected in some way. ✷

LUKE: At a basketball game, I would sometimes look up at the 5,000-6,000 people in the stands, and think about how I probably knew the stories of eighty percent of the people in attendance.

The intimacy of Washington is a breath of fresh air.

Wilda was also an instructional assistant for special education and an alternative education aide at Washington High School, and since Lorri was a secretary in the high school's athletic office, they were around each other quite a bit. Throw basketball into the mix, too, and they had a lot in common. They developed a strong friendship.

Lorri learned that Wilda was an eclectic woman. She was an interior decorator on the side who enjoyed collecting Jewel Tea and Candlewick antique dishes. She loved shopping, and Coach Omer oftentimes joked that their basement was a store in itself. He called it "Wilda-Mart." She was a bargain shopper, and she bought anything she thought might be needed in the future. She had an entire "gift closet" dedicated to special occasions for her friends and family members. Whenever something exciting arose, she would simply take an item from her closet of gifts and give it to the person immediately. This, like her bus routine with Luke, describes her selflessness and kindness.

By the time Luke was a senior, however, Luke was the one helping Wilda onto the team bus. It was as if everything had come full circle. Years before, she had been diagnosed with breast cancer, and her illness had taken a turn for the worse by the time her husband entered his final year of coaching at Washington in 2005. She had become terribly frail and weak as the disease tried to crush her. She never lost her uplifting attitude and positive spirit, however. After one of her chemotherapy treatments, she once showed up at Washington High School wearing a blonde wig (not her natural hair color), and said to Lorri, "I always heard that blondes have more fun."

All in all, it was a taxing season on Coach Omer. He would oftentimes spend the entire day in Indianapolis at the hospital with her, make the two-hour drive to Washington for a basketball game that night, then drive back up to Indianapolis after the game to be with her again and sleep at the bedside of his spouse of forty-one years.

Basketball, however, was also perhaps his escape from a world of pain. Especially in 2005. Despite the tumultuous storm he and Wilda were enduring, the Hatchets were lighting up the hardwood, falling only twice in the regular season.

At the start of the season, the Hatchets' small forward Justin Smith had jokingly pointed up into the rafters while they were stretching before practice, noticing there was nowhere to hang another banner.

"Coach," he laughed, "if we win State this year, where will the banner go?"

Considering they hadn't won a Sectional in twenty-two years, there was a chuckle at the mere mention of the word "State." It was difficult enough just to get past their arch-rival, Vincennes Lincoln, in the Sectional.

State seemed implausible, but so did a Sectional championship considering their wretched post-season history. Washington's mantra for the season became "Just Believe" as Coach Omer tried to fuel their mentalities with the positive idea they could go as far as they wanted to go—they had all the talent in the world to win a Sectional. Their motto also took on a religious meaning for many of the players.

All season, the Hatchet House was electric. You started to wonder why it wasn't constructed big enough to fit the entire town. Several years prior, the girls' games had more fans and energy swarming around the program. Now, the excitement for boys' basketball had finally returned to Washington.

We had no idea what to make of it all. The attention that basketball brought our family was something we never could have fathomed. We were just like any other family. I was a working-class father, a plant manager at Perdue Foods, and Lorri was a working-class mother, a secretary in Washington's athletic department. We lived in a two-story, four-bedroom house in the Washington countryside, and we ate dinner together as a family in the evening. There was nothing special about us. Yet, because Luke was tall and good at basketball, our last name was in the limelight. This is another reason why we taught our children about the importance of their reputations and character: You never know when your time will come. You never know when your name will be exposed.

The Hatchets defeated Gibson Southern 70-51 in the first round of the Sectional, setting up a matchup against Vincennes Lincoln in the Sectional Final. It had become quite a routine, unfortunately, for the Lincoln Alices of Vincennes (that's right, the Alices—from the title of the classic 1900 novel *Alice of Old Vincennes*) to ruin our Sectional dreams. Luke's sophomore year, they defeated Washington

54-48 in the regular season and 55-51 in the Sectional Final. Luke's junior year, they defeated Washington 46-35 in the regular season and 64-54 in the Sectional Final. They were our arch-rival and our Achilles' heel. No matter how successful our regular season was, they always seemed to come along and spoil our postseason. Not to mention, the Hatchets had hit a wall in Sectionals for the past two decades. Our recent Sectional history was discussed among Hatchets fans much like the World Series among Chicago Cubs fans. With bitterness. With anxiety. With disdain.

The 2005 season, however, was different. After defeating Vincennes Lincoln in the regular season 66-60, we (finally) knocked them out in the postseason, destroying them 83-60—Washington's first Sectional title in twenty-two years. I'd be lying if I said that one didn't feel especially satisfying.

Following the final buzzer, Hatchet fans flooded the floor, and Lorri remembers hugging Justin Smith and congratulating him. "We're not done yet," Justin told her. ✷

That evening, the team boarded a fire truck and rode around town (though it was freezing cold) as the driver blared its sirens. Washingtonites excitedly lined up on the streets as the fire truck made its way through the town. The bars emptied out. People came outside and

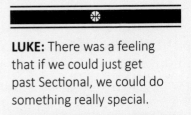

LUKE: There was a feeling that if we could just get past Sectional, we could do something really special.

cheered from their porches. A local farmer named Tom Boyd organized a gigantic bonfire for the entire town in the parking lot of an old, abandoned Kmart building. The fire was so large it completely melted the blacktop.

After advancing from a Sectional as difficult as ours, the floodgates seemed to open up. At Regionals in the Hatchet House, Washington crushed Edgewood 72-33 in the first round in the morning and then took care of Scottsburg 88-68 in the final round that night—not a bad day at the office. Considering Scottsburg ran the Grinnell offense, a high-tempo style of basketball where a shot was usually taken within the first ten seconds of any given possession, holding them to sixty-eight points was downright remarkable.

Again, the team boarded a Washington fire truck and blared its sirens, and Tom Boyd hosted another bonfire. Because it was so cold, some of the players actually got ill from riding the fire truck around town through the frigid, Hoosier winter.

Approaching the Semi-State game in Seymour, Coach Omer approached the only two freshmen on the team—Tyler (our son) and Kyle Price—and told them that he was allowed to dress only one of them for their semi-final matchup against Indianapolis Roncalli. If they won Semi-State, he told them, he would dress the other one for the State game. He said it was up to them who dressed each game.

It didn't matter much because they never played, but it was more about having the honor to sit on the bench. Tyler, honestly, wasn't a great player as a freshman. Luke, even as a freshman, was light years ahead of Tyler in both basketball IQ and skill. ✹

Tyler asked Luke if he should dress in Semi-State.

"Let Kyle dress the Semi-State game," Luke said confidently, "because we're going to State."

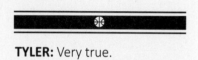

TYLER: Very true.

Luke was right. In a much closer game, they knocked out Roncalli, 51-46, in the one-game Semi-State in Seymour, and, just like that, after seemingly being cursed in Sectionals for two decades, Washington High School had jumped all the way to the Indiana Class 3A State Finals, set to play against Plymouth High School at Conseco Fieldhouse, the Indianapolis home of the NBA's Indiana Pacers.

After Washington's victory over Roncalli, law enforcement from surrounding towns—Bedford, Shoals, Loogootee, and Montgomery—escorted the Hatchet bus all the way back to Washington. This is how big a deal high school basketball is in southern Indiana—law enforcement from *other* towns were involved. When the team got back to Washington, they, again, boarded a Washington fire truck and rode it around town. Tom Boyd hosted another bonfire.

That poor parking lot.

Never in my life had I seen Washington more excited and united. All you had to do was drive down Main Street and notice the variation of "Go Hatchets!" signs in every window of each restaurant or boutique, or the gigantic "Luke Zeller for Mr. Basketball" sign towering above a Washington plaza or the "Beat Plymouth!" sign outside the White Steamer, a famous burger joint in the town. Every business seemed to show its support in some way. Even the churches had signs. Parents and businesses purchased "Good Luck" ads in the local newspaper, the *Washington Times-Herald,* and a Washington-based band recorded a ballad called "The Hatchet Song." The chorus went like this:

We are the Hatchets of Wash-ing-ton!
The Mighty Hatchets of Wash-ing-ton!
Going to Indy, Gonna get 'er done,
Oh, yeah! The Black and Gold!

Since starting a bonfire on the streets of Indianapolis at the State championship wouldn't paint Washington in the most positive light, Tom Boyd had an alternative idea. He had a semi-trailer made with Washington's team picture on its side and a peel-off sticker that changed "State Finalists" to "State Champions" in case they won. This trailer became the gathering place for Washingtonites in downtown Indy.

But it wasn't easy.

Tom had to go through Washington's state representative and the City of Indianapolis to get permission to park the trailer across from Conseco. "I don't care what it costs," he told them. "I need to be able to park that semi across the street from Conseco Fieldhouse."

He ended up renting a space across from Conseco for the weekend of the State championship game just to park the semi. They blasted "The Hatchet Song" continually from gigantic speakers on top of the trailer. We looked like a bunch of country folk who had never been to a big city before—and we were throwing a big party to celebrate.

Fans showed up throughout the weekend in waves, following each other from Washington to Indianapolis, through rich Indiana farmland, their cars decked out in window chalk and paint in support of the Hatchets.

If you had visited Washington the weekend of the State championship game, you would have thought you were walking through a ghost town. You could have robbed an entire neighborhood or street of businesses without anyone catching you. The town was virtually vacant.

And the best thing about playing at Conseco was that there was finally enough space to fit the entire town.

※

Wilda Omer was in attendance at the State championship game. As weak as her body was, it was as if God was using the gift of basketball to strengthen her heart, fuel her will, and allow her to get lost in a world of joy and hope through sport.

It was certainly a game to get lost in.

With 1.8 seconds left in overtime, Plymouth led Washington 72-71. Plymouth had just taken the lead, and Washington had blown a twelve-point lead in the fourth quarter. The Plymouth fans were going crazy and were in the process of passing out their State championship T-shirts. Washingtonites were completely deflated.

It was Washington's ball on the baseline on the opposite end, and Coach Omer called a timeout, mostly to try to convince the officials there should be more time on the clock. He didn't have any luck, however, and the Hatchets took the floor with a chance to run one final play.

Lorri and I looked nervously at each other. Cody and Lorri's father were sitting with us, as well.

"1.8 seconds isn't much time," Lorri said to me.

"It's just enough time to 'catch and shoot,'" I said to her.

Once the players took the floor, however, Plymouth's Hall of Fame head coach Jack Edison studied Washington's inbound formation and called his own timeout. This actually played to Washington's advantage because they hadn't had much time to set something up in the previous timeout. ❈

The Hatchets took the floor.

Luke later told us that he wanted to take the shot because he didn't want the likely miss and loss to be on any of his teammates' shoulders. He knew he would have other op-

LUKE: The plan was for me to get a screen underneath the basket and attempt a three-pointer from the opposite wing. It was a play we had ran

119

plenty of times in practice.

"Just give me the ball, and I'll score," I said.

It's difficult to explain, but I felt a sense of peace about the whole thing.

Before we took the floor, Coach Omer pulled me aside and told me, "Don't heave that thing up there; take a dribble, and get your feet set."

As I took the floor, I prayed, "God, if this is it and we lose, let me be able to glorify You. No matter what, let me glorify You."

Finally, I prayed, "But if you could do something cool, that'd be fun."

LUKE: Plymouth's timeout not only helped us because we were out of timeouts, but also helped because of the changes they made. Whereas before the timeout they had a player defending the inbounds pass, after the timeout they didn't. This gave Justin more room to make the pass. When I caught the ball, though, I didn't realize how far out I was. I just felt I needed to keep running toward the ball until I got open.

---

portunities beyond high school basketball, and he didn't want one of his teammates to have to live with potentially missing a buzzer-beater in the State championship for the rest of his life. Rather, he wanted to be the one that dealt with the potential consequences and humiliation.

The ref handed Justin the ball, a second or two passed, and Justin threw an overhead soccer-style pass (Justin was also a soccer player) to Luke just inside midcourt.

Luke turned, took one dribble, advanced across half court, and threw up a surprisingly normal-looking jump shot, considering he was more than forty-five-feet out.

Swish.

He drained it.

Washington: 74.

Plymouth: 72.

Luke's teammates climbed all over him—half the crowd devastated, the other half roaring, and *all* of the crowd shocked. Minutes before, Plymouth fans were the ecstatic ones and Washington fans were silent. Now, the entire mood inside Conseco flip-flopped.

Euphoria ensued.

All I could do was hug Lorri. It was neat to witness Cody's excitement as well, and I think it helped plant a seed in him for the future. Washington had just earned its first

State championship since 1942, and it had been one of the most memorable finishes in Indiana's legend-filled basketball history.

As Luke's teammates hugged him, he looked as if he was in a daze—and maybe he was. He looked up toward the ceiling expressionless, both of his hands raised, and pointed toward the heavens.

This made me most proud.

The image of him pointing upward, in my opinion, was a perfect representation of Luke. After hitting one of the most miraculous shots in State Finals history, his first instinct wasn't to glorify himself, nor to even celebrate with his teammates, but rather point toward the heavens and give glory to God. His immediate response in a moment of elation was worship. I always found this both encouraging and inspiring. ❄

Following the game, the IH-SAA welcomed Washington's team to the podium to give them their State championship medals (their rings would be delivered later). On the medal stand with the team was Wilda. She hugged her husband and was also given a medal—it was a beautiful moment.

LUKE: That's some of the best worship with God I have ever experienced. It was all about having a platform to glorify God, win or lose.

After forty years of coaching, Coach Omer had finally won a State championship, and he retired in the coming weeks. Wilda passed away five months later after her long, painful battle with cancer. It was terribly sad, but at the same time, if 2005 was going to be her last year on earth, I can't think of a better year for her to experience alongside her husband.

A week or two after the State championship game, Coach Omer hosted a team banquet for the players and parents. At the end of the banquet, several pictures were taken of the team next to their new State championship banner. Wilda was in every picture . . . next to her husband . . . and also next to Luke.

At one point, she reached over and grabbed Luke's hand, just like eleven years before. It was a moment that Luke will never forget.

I think Luke learned a lot from his miracle buzzer-beater, which was soon heralded as "The Shot." And, as usual, I also think I learned a lot from Luke.

It's fascinating how sports have the ability to point people toward something that transcends themselves. In his reaction to The Shot, in his interviews after the victory, and in his conversations with us that evening, it was never about him. It was about his team, and, most important, it was about God. Thing is, I believe he would have had the same reaction if they had lost. Win or lose, I think he would have viewed the journey as a *gift* from God. Even if they had lost to Vincennes Lincoln in the Sectional Final for the third year in a row, I know he would have still viewed his high school career and the times he had at Washington as nothing less than a gift. Luke was as competitive as they come, but his identity was always rooted in something much stronger than basketball. Basketball was merely an opportunity to proclaim what he was really about.

This later became one of the foundational principles for DistinX-ion, the basketball ministry he founded, where sports is used as an avenue for both teaching character and challenging people to contemplate life's biggest questions. I was more proud of him for giving glory to God than I was of him for making the shot that won them a State championship. His reaction to it all, I believe, revealed where his heart, mind, and true identity were placed.

I find all of this important in parenting, too—using different activities, like sports, as tools to teach character. If character is the thread to every activity your children participate in, they will be more concerned with their conduct than their performance. And one of the ways you teach this, I believe, is raising them to believe in something that is bigger than themselves.

Rick Warren starts his bestselling book *The Purpose Driven Life* with the phrase, "It's not about you," and as your children become young adults and develop their worldview, I think it is vital that you raise them to believe in something that does not begin or end with themselves or their performance, though this is the way most of the world acts. Their self-worth must derive from something much more constant than the things they do in this world.

Of course, this cannot be forced upon your children, but it can be modeled for your children. A father who returns home after a frustrating day at work, disgruntled and testy, may not be modeling a deeper-rooted identity for his children. A mother enveloped in drama or gossip with other parents on the team may not be modeling a deeper-rooted identity for her children. Attitudes like these reflect an identity and purpose tossed in the inconsistencies of the changing winds of this world. Children are perceptive beings. It is as if their subconscious is continually taking notes. However, isn't it possible that your consistency in your actions and parenting can allude to the deeper-rooted identity you have already attained?

Just as Luke's reaction to The Shot reflected his deeper-rooted identity, we soon learned why it is so important to have an identity that goes beyond what you do, an identity with the framework of integrity that breaches into eternity.

Immediately following the State championship game, our family piled into our vehicle and made the three-hour drive up to South Bend for the McDonald's All-American game, which was taking place on Wednesday. Luke's invitation to play in the prestigious game had come weeks before and called for him to get there on Saturday, impossible obviously because of the State championship (you know, one of those games Coach Omer didn't want him to miss). The team celebrated. The town celebrated. But we left Conseco and went straight to South Bend. There was no time to rest. No time to even see a replay of The Shot (this was before the days of smartphones and 4G networks). It wasn't until Sunday morning that we finally saw a replay of The Shot on *SportsCenter's* daily Top 10 plays. ESPN analyst Jay Bilas called our son "Cool-hand Luke."

The week of the All-American game, however, it was as if the day before never happened. Suddenly, Luke was just another player. It didn't matter that he won an Indiana Class 3A title. It didn't matter he hit one of the most fabled shots in Indiana State championship history. He was a giant among giants. He was a great player, sure, but so was everyone else. After reaching the mountaintop a day before, he suddenly blended in. I think it was a humbling experience for him and a poignant reminder of the fleeting nature of fame.

Not to mention because he showed up late, Luke missed getting his measurements taken for his warm-up sweats. So, since he wasn't there, they guessed on his measurements. The result was a pair of sweats that were three sizes too big. As his team warmed up before the McDonald's All-American game, Luke looked like Ronald McDonald out there. ✱

His reaction to The Shot showed everyone that his worth was not in basketball, and the McDonald's All-American game showed him why it didn't make sense to put his worth in basketball. Overall, the whole experience was a reminder to Lorri and me that if basketball continued to play a major role in our lives as Tyler and Cody grew older, it'd be important for us to gently guide them toward a foundation beyond the hardwood.

LUKE: My pants were so baggy I thought I was going to trip while going through the layup line. My sleeves were so huge it felt like I was wearing a robe.

Perhaps one of the best examples of a sound identity and foundation is John Wooden, the late UCLA basketball coach and Hoosier native whose Bruin teams won ten NCAA titles. And it was also at the McDonald's All-American game that we interacted with John Wooden for the first time. I was predictably star-struck.

Coach Wooden had heard about The Shot and requested to meet Luke when we first arrived in South Bend—the two of them met during Luke's first day with the team at practice. I probably asked Luke a thousand questions about what it was like to meet him, probing for every last detail all the way down to the firmness of his handshake. Obviously, Luke thought it was cool. But he hadn't seen Coach Wooden win all those championships like I had. I was pretty jealous that Luke had not only met John Wooden but had also been *complimented* by John Wooden on the shot he made and the season he had.

Coach Omer was granted the opportunity to meet Coach Wooden that same day. At one point, Coach Wooden looked at Coach Omer and stated, "You know, I won ten national championship rings." Coach Wooden paused. "But I would give you two of my national championship rings for a State championship ring in Indiana."

I think Coach Omer walked away from that conversation feeling pretty good. He had something John Wooden didn't have, and, not just that, but he had something that John Wooden *wanted.* I'm unsure how I would have responded if I were Coach Omer.

Then, on Monday morning (the All-American game was on Wednesday), I was down in the hotel lobby with Tyler and Cody eating breakfast. We had been sitting and eating for a few minutes when Cody, who was in sixth grade at the time, pointed behind me and said, "Isn't that someone famous?"

I spun around and saw Coach Wooden sitting at a table right behind me with his family. He must have just walked into the lobby.

Wide-eyed, I spun back around and looked across the table at Tyler and Cody. "Okay guys, we're going to remain calm," I said, probably talking more to myself than either of the boys. "He's with his family," I continued, "so it's probably best not to bother him."

We finished our breakfast, and, admittedly, I tried to make eye contact with him as I walked by his table, but I resisted the temptation to say anything. I walked past him and looked back over my shoulder at the boys. That's when I saw Coach Wooden stop them. Tyler didn't say anything to him. Cody didn't say anything to him. It was Coach Wooden, of all people, who said something to *them.*

"Tell me who you boys are," Wooden said curiously, as I watched from a distance. They explained to him that they were Luke's brothers, and for the next ten minutes, Coach Wooden asked Tyler and Cody questions about themselves—their grade, their school, their home. ✹

Over the next two days, Tyler, Cody, and I started scheming on how we might be able to meet Coach Wooden again and get his

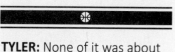

TYLER: None of it was about him.

autograph. I had purchased one of his books in the hotel bookstore and had decided in my mind that I wanted a signed John Wooden book.

We started spending countless hours in the lobby, asking hotel employees about his whereabouts, and searching the hotel for him. Practically stalking him. Okay, we were stalking him. ✳

It was mostly just Cody and me. Tyler never really cared about celebrities. Even when he visited the White House and met the President of the United States later in his life, the only thing he had to say about

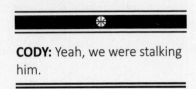

CODY: Yeah, we were stalking him.

the experience was, "It's just a bunch of old stuff there." Still, Tyler helped us in our stalking efforts because it was a task to accomplish.

"You guys have been spending a lot of time in the lobby of the hotel," Lorri had said to me one day. "What are you waiting for?"

I told her, and she rolled her eyes.

⚜

On Tuesday, we spotted Coach Wooden in the hotel lobby signing autographs next to Morgan Wootten, the winningest head coach in the history of high school basketball.

This, we knew, was our chance.

We walked past Coach Wooden and Coach Wootten to get in line.

"Cody!" Coach Wooden said.

I'm not sure I can explain in words what was going on in my mind. All I could think was: *John Wooden just called my son by his name.*

Cody turned around.

"Cody, come here," he waved.

Cody walked over and stood next to him.

"I want you to stand right here," he said.

I studied the scene, and I was thoroughly confused. What was going on?

They kept chitchatting for a few minutes, and it soon became apparent that Coach Wooden was having Cody stand next to him to block the sun that was shining through the window and into Coach

Wooden's eyes.

Cody made eye contact with me and innocently shrugged.

Once the book signing was over, Coach Wooden gave Cody a note that read, "Be quick but don't hurry." I got my book signed, too, and finally got to shake the hand of a legend. We asked Tyler if he wanted Coach Wooden's autograph, and all he said was, "No, not really."

\wwww/

After Luke helped Washington win its first State championship in sixty-three years and became the school's first Indiana Mr. Basketball award winner since Steve Bouchie in 1979, many people said something to us along the lines of, "Boy, it's really going to be tough on Tyler after what Luke accomplished."

Truthfully, we weren't sure if Tyler would be a good basketball player or even enjoy the game to the extent that Luke did. I sort of believed the magical 2005 season and Luke's basketball success might be a one-time thing. After all, Luke showed a lot of desire in junior high; Tyler did not. Luke grew early on; Tyler did not. Luke got a lot of playing time as a freshman and started every game; Tyler did not. The only reason Tyler even dressed for the State championship game is because he took a risk and let Kyle Price dress for the Semi-State game.

There was a picture taken by the *Indianapolis Star,* however, that I think describes the situation perfectly. It's my favorite picture of all time. The photograph was snapped immediately after Luke hit the buzzer-beater in the State championship game. Luke has his hands raised, pointing toward the heavens, his eyes doing the same, as senior Justin Smith hugs him from the front and senior Isaac Stoll wraps his arms around him from behind. Three seniors. Three starters. All celebrating the crowning achievement of their high school careers.

There's another player in the picture, however, screaming and celebrating just to the right of Luke, who could easily be overlooked. It's Tyler. He is significantly shorter than Luke and looks far less mature, almost as if Coach Omer allowed a junior high student to sit on the bench for the game. Unlike the other three guys in the picture who are celebrating in their jerseys, Tyler fades into the background, wearing his gold, Hatchet warm-up shirt.

Looking back, it's ironic—a hint of foreshadowing, perhaps, as if the picture is trying to tell its viewers: *There's more to come.*

\\⅄⅄//

From the Background, to the Forefront

When Luke graduated, Tyler blossomed. Tyler would be the first to tell you that he wasn't a good basketball player as a freshman. But somewhere along the line over the next few years, the team became his. Everything was handed down, just as the *Indianapolis Star* photograph foreshadowed.

Much of it, I believe, had to do with the coaching. ✹

Upon Coach Omer's retirement following the 2005 State championship, Hatchet fans immediately knew that the hiring of Gene Miiller (yes, that's the correct spelling) as athletic director and head basketball coach at Washington High School would help us build on Coach Omer's previous success.

Before arriving in Washington, Coach Miiller had coached five years at Kankakee Valley, seventeen at Vincennes Lincoln, and seven at Lafayette Jeff. He was known for his relentlessness and work ethic. Without a doubt, he was one of the most respected coaches in the state.

TYLER: Just as Luke really connected with Coach Omer, I really connected with our new coach, Gene Miiller. He was someone I respected greatly. He laid the foundation for me that Coach Williams was able to build on once I went to UNC.

Bill Richardson—a former sports editor for the *Washington Times Herald* who covered Coach Miiller's Vincennes Lincoln teams while working at the *Vincennes Sun-Commercial*—in a published quote, called the hiring of Coach Miiller the fifth-greatest day in Hatchet history, the first four being their State championships in 1930, 1941, 1942, and 2005. In three decades of coaching, Coach Miiller was yet to win a State championship (though his Alices of Vincennes

Lincoln did reach the State championship game in 1984)—but that was about to change.

Coach Miiller helped strengthen Tyler's psyche, giving him the confidence to eventually become a leader for the Hatchets, and strengthened his physique by stressing the importance of hitting the weight room in the offseason. This all helped him eventually become a go-to scorer for the Hatchets. Coach Miiller always used to say, "If my best player is my best worker, then I've got a basketball team." Under Coach Miiller's leadership, Tyler became both of these.

Another player who really developed at Washington was a six foot eleven post player in Tyler's grade named Seth Coy. Seth was Tyler's best friend and a fan favorite. The two of them on the hardwood became known as the "Twin Towers" because of their dominance in the post.

TYLER: Of course, growing an entire foot helped me get better, as well.

Seth's rise in the basketball ranks is one of the greatest underdog stories I've ever heard.

To begin, Seth had an array of odd, health-related issues. In high school, he was already on his third set of teeth—they would just fall out. I never understood what exactly it was that he had, but his physical differences never seemed to bother him. One year, his teeth were falling out again, and I asked him, "Seth, what are you going to do?" He shrugged, smiled, and replied, "Well, they'll grow back."

Growing up, he had weak, large joints and grew faster and earlier than most of his peers. Doctors tested him for different abnormalities but never diagnosed him with anything specific.

I remember taking note of Seth as he was coming up through junior high and believing that all he needed was a chance. He wasn't very coordinated, but he had potential. I helped him with his shot and some of basketball's fundamentals, even something as simple as a right-handed layup. He would also come with us to AAU tournaments and stay with us in our hotel room—we loved being with him.

Once he got to high school, Coach Miiller also believed in him and helped take his game to the next level. Seth kept growing, sprouting up to nearly seven feet, though his father was five foot five and his mother was five foot four. They had to place a special order for his size twenty-one shoes.

Neither Seth nor Tyler played a single varsity game their freshman year, but they steadily improved as they ventured through high school. Seth went from averaging 1.7 points per game his sophomore season and 1.3 points per game his junior season to *13.6 points and 9.6 rebounds per game* his senior season. He exploded. ✹

He came out of nowhere. One game, he set a school record with twenty-six rebounds.

Tyler averaged 14.9 points and 8.1 rebounds per game his sophomore season, then 18.3 points and 9.5 rebounds per game his junior season, and 33.1 points and 11.0 rebounds per game his senior season.

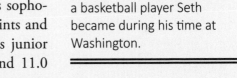

TYLER: It's really hard to put into words how much better a basketball player Seth became during his time at Washington.

The two of them really made each other better basketball players. It's hard to tell if Tyler would be the player he is today if it wasn't for Seth. ✹

They would walk off the floor after practice and have scratches and bruises all over them. They beat the tar out of one another. Seth knew exactly how to get in Tyler's head, and he would do it to make Tyler

TYLER: I know he made me into the player I am today.

stronger. After practice, however, they would walk off the floor as best friends again. ✹

No one had a better attitude about life than Seth. He seemed to make an impact on everyone, whether it was the community's most important leaders or a drug dealer in the trailer park. His sense of humor and the joy he carried through life was refreshing to everyone who interacted with him. In basketball practice, Tyler says his timing was

CODY: I know that when I was a freshman I would rather have guarded Tyler in practice then Seth. Seth was so strong and relentless. When he was on the court he would have a jersey full of blood from his braces going through his lip, and he would be yelling at guys to play better. I know that he brought out the best in everyone on our team and set an example of what hard work looked like. Looking back, he really taught me a lot about what it took to improve and become successful.

After practice, however, he could flip the switch better than anyone that I've been with. He was pure entertainment. He was always making funny jokes and brightening the day of everyone around him.

impeccable when it came to cracking a joke or lightening the mood if things grew too intense. At basketball camp, kids would climb all over him like he was a tree. After basketball games, he loved talking to parents and fans, and, of course, kids. He was a leader, role model, and inspiration—mature beyond his years. Seth spent a lot of time at our house and, at times, seemed part of our family.

By the time Seth and Tyler were seniors, after falling in Regionals the previous two seasons, the Hatchets once again had ambitions to do something special. Teams had no idea how to defend against the "Twin Towers."

From wrestling with physical abnormalities to being one of the key ingredients on Washington's 2008 team, Seth inspired everyone to keep living, despite life's challenges.

Before we knew it, the Hatchets were making another deep postseason run, just like Luke's senior season. ✼

The biggest challenge in the postseason was their Regional tournament, which was loaded with talent, featuring No. 1-ranked Evansville Memorial and No. 2-ranked Edgewood—the top two teams in the state. (Washington was ranked No. 4 in the state.)

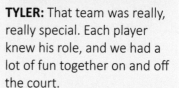

TYLER: That team was really, really special. Each player knew his role, and we had a lot of fun together on and off the court.

Unfortunately, the night before, Tyler had contracted the flu, and struggled to feel any better the day of Regionals. On quite possibly the most challenging day of basketball Washington had ever seen, Tyler, their leading scorer, had a stomach virus.

In the morning, Washington defeated No. 2 Edgewood 70-63, and Evansville Memorial crushed tenth-ranked Charlestown 64-50, setting up a No. 1 (Evansville Memorial) vs. No. 4 (Washington) matchup that evening.

In between the morning and evening Regional games, the team had a tradition of going back to Coach Miiller's house—basically to quarantine them from the community and the hype. Tyler, still sick, spent most of the time sleeping. ✦

That evening was the fullest I've ever seen the Hatchet House. It was standing room only, and a fire marshal eventually had to close the gates and make sure no one else entered the stadium.

Before the game, one of Washington's managers approached Lorri and loudly asked, "Do you have any Imodium? Tyler has diarrhea!" Our whole section probably heard him.

Judging by his performance, however, you never would have

TYLER: I spent the entire afternoon curled up, sleeping in Coach Miiller's bed. I was knocked out for three hours. I was happy I wasn't throwing up, and I just hoped I would feel well enough to play that evening and have the opportunity to produce something for the team.

known Tyler was sick. He scored 38 points and grabbed 17 rebounds as Washington ran over the best team in the state, 84-65. After tallying 32 points and 19 rebounds that morning, Tyler totaled 70 points and 36 boards on the day.

Perhaps he should've played sick more often.

After knocking off the two top-ranked teams in the state in a single day, Washington continued rolling through the postseason, slipping by Batesville in Semi-State 73-69 to advance to the Class 3A State championship for the first time since Luke's senior year.

The excitement and buzz from three years prior once again returned. Tom Boyd had another semi-trailer designed, featuring a picture of the 2008 team on its side, and rented the same parking spots across from Conseco. Another rendition of "The Hatchet Song" was made, and the signs once again went up around the town. One weekend, Roy Williams and the University of North Carolina coaches visited Washington and saw Tyler's name on a sign above the local liquor store. We hoped they didn't think Tyler was a loyal customer.

In the State championship, Seth and Tyler couldn't be stopped, and it was never a close matchup as Washington defeated Fort Wayne Harding 84-60. Tyler set an overall State championship game record with 43 points and a game-high 16 rebounds while Seth added 20 points and 16 rebounds. Tyler, strangely, scored more points than Brownsburg's team totaled in its 40-39 4A State championship victory over Marion High School that same weekend, a game won on a last-second shot by future Butler University and NBA star Gordon Hayward. ❋

Much like how the magic of the State championship game Luke's senior year perfectly described the 2005 season, the State championship game in 2008 very much described the season because of Tyler and Seth's dominance.

It was awesome to watch Tyler and Seth hoist the trophy, to think about how far each of them had come—especially Seth. I knew they'd be friends for life, and it would be their State championship rings that would forever bind them. That April, Tyler was also named Indiana Mr. Basketball, but even that, we knew, was a tribute to Tyler and Seth's work ethic and how they both made each other better on the basketball floor.

CODY: After Luke won his State championship, someone asked Tyler, "Are you going to lead your team to State and win on a dramatic half-court shot with 1.8 seconds left?!" Tyler said, "Nope, I'm just going to win by twenty. No half-court shot needed." That's exactly what happened. Actually, we won by twenty-four.

Seth received a Division I scholarship to East Tennessee State University in Johnson City, Tennessee. It was amazing to see how far he had come. His hard work and positive attitude proved to everyone that no circumstance or stroke of bad luck can stop you from attaining your dreams. Now, he had a State championship ring on his finger and a letter of commitment to ETSU. He was also named prom king the spring of his senior year. ✿

The following summer in late July, Tyler had just returned to Washington after his freshman year at the University of North Carolina when we received a phone call from Coach Miiller's daughter, Hanna.

TYLER: To celebrate, he wore his big, purple king hat to school the next day. Seth just made everyone smile. It seemed like he never had a bad day.

Lorri answered the phone and heard Hanna on the other end, but she was crying so hard that Lorri couldn't understand her. All Lorri could decipher were four haunting words: "Seth has been killed."

Minutes later, Tyler got the same phone call. We soon learned the details: Seth had been driving through Shelby County in Kentucky on his way back home to Indiana after his first year at ETSU (down the same highway Tyler had traveled hours before on his way back from college) when his car hydroplaned and flipped. Seth, who wasn't wearing a seat belt, was ejected from the vehicle.

Tyler didn't say much to us. All he said was, "I'm going over to Cody Lee's." Cody Lee was another senior on the 2008 State championship team, and their entire title team was gathering at his house to support one another. Tyler returned home at about one o'clock in the morning, extremely quiet. Only Tyler knows what Tyler was thinking.

Seth's memorial was held in the Hatchet House, and I can't think of a better place to have held it. Basketball brought everyone in Washington, Indiana together—and so did Seth. Basketball provided Hatchet fans with hope, joy, and inspiration—and so did Seth. No one could be a better representation of Hatchet Hoops than Seth Coy. The day of his memorial, the Hatchet House was so packed, anyone driving by probably wondered if the Sectional was moved to early August. Basketball impacted the entire town—and so did Seth.

There was such a diverse crowd in the Hatchet House that day. Young. Old. Rich. Poor. Teams from different towns. People who lived in Washington that we hadn't seen in twenty years, but had apparently been influenced by Seth.

At the memorial, Coach Miiller stood at the podium and said, "I'll remember Seth for his zest for life, for his sense of humor—who could ever forget his sense of humor?—that deep voice that he had, his love for children . . . every time after the game, he was just swamped by children."

When Tyler got married in the summer of 2014, I couldn't help but look at his groomsmen standing next to him and picture Seth there, too.

TYLER: He would have been standing up there next to me.

Declaration of an Era

I remember a time when Luke was a freshman in high school. He was having a good season and was on pace to score the most points as a freshman in Washington High School history. Cody (a third grader), Tyler (a sixth grader), and Luke were sitting out in our sunroom flipping through Washington's basketball record book.

"I just hope you guys set the records high," Cody said to them, "so it's a challenge for me when I come along and break them."

Luke later came into the kitchen and said to Lorri and me, "You won't ever believe what Cody just said."

CODY: I think this story has developed over the years. This is *actually* what happened: Luke, Tyler, and I were flipping through a yearbook, and Luke and Tyler were pointing out the girls that they found attractive. I told them, "My wife is going to be hotter than *both* of yours."

But yeah, I wanted to break their records, too.

Coach Miiller and the team decided to dedicate the upcoming 2010 season, Cody's junior year, to Seth. Each player wore a #42 patch on the left side of his jersey throughout the season in tribute

to Seth, and a number of things were done at the Hatchet House throughout the year to celebrate the inspiring, albeit brief, life that he lived.

Of course, by this point, an obvious trend had developed. Washington won a State championship when Luke was a senior (Tyler was a freshman), another State championship when Tyler was a senior (Cody was a freshman), and Cody had a chance to do the same. Really, he was *expected* to do the same. Like Tyler following Luke, people said, "Boy, it's really going to be tough on Cody after what Luke *and* Tyler accomplished." But Washington's recent success had truly become an era of sorts, and people had grown to expect State championships, as crazy as that sounds.

Cody's laid-back personality allowed him to handle the "pressure" perfectly. He was simply playing basketball. He never got too worked up about anything. Luke takes control of situations. Tyler internalizes situations. Cody just rolls with situations. One of his math teachers at Washington, Kevin Stallman, put it best in regard to the boy's personalities in the context of the classroom: Luke wanted to help his classmates with their homework, Tyler just wanted the lecture to end so he could get his homework done, and Cody didn't care about the process as long as he got an A. Their personalities are very distinct. ✽

Still, because it was only Cody's junior season, most fans didn't expect Washington to accomplish what it had in 2008. It wouldn't have fit the "win State when the Zeller brother is a senior" trend. Plus, most would agree that the 2010 team wasn't as talented as the State championship teams in 2005 and 2008.

But the 2010 Hatchets played the entire season inspired in memory of Seth Coy. The season transcended sports, much like Luke's senior year when they won a State title for Coach Omer and his cancer-stricken wife.

There was a sense that they were en route to something special,

TYLER: Mom and Dad always say that within the first five minutes of meeting someone, Luke knows everything about the person, I usually don't last the five minutes, and Cody is trying to pull a prank on the person. Luke is the talker. Cody is the prankster.

as they won their first twelve games of the season. Despite not being as talented offensively as past teams, the Hatchets played gritty man-to-man defense throughout the season and shut teams down defensively. They wore everyone down. I truly believe they had to have been one of the best-conditioned teams in the state because of Coach Miiller, and they would often times pull ahead of teams in the fourth quarter simply because they weren't as fatigued.

In the postseason, the Hatchets fought their way to the State championship game with scrappy defense, holding their first five tournament opponents to an average of 39 points. And, once again, the traditions continued—the bonfires, the trailer, the invasion of the block across from Conseco, the song, and the thousands of Hatchet fans traveling to Indianapolis. Our players made it clear to the media before the State championship game against Gary Wallace that they wanted to win the title for Seth Coy. He was their rallying cry and their drive.

And they did.

The Hatchets defeated Gary Wallace in overtime, 65-62, their sixth State championship in the school's treasured history, and third title in five years. Cody tied a State-title record in rebounding with 26 rebounds (also tying Seth Coy's school record) and added 20 points, going against a strong Wallace front line featuring future Michigan State star Branden Dawson. ✳

In the postgame press conference, Gary Wallace head coach Renaldo Thomas was quoted saying, "I hope there won't be any more Zellers."

He has Lorri to thank for that one. She locked the bull up early. ✳

CODY: I knew I had a lot of rebounds during the game, but I didn't know that I had tied a school record. I remember one of the reporters asking me after the game what I thought about tying Seth Coy for the school record of 26 rebounds in a game. It just sent a chill down my back. Getting 26 rebounds was neat, but to share the record with Seth and share that connection with someone who means so much to me is something that I'll never forget.

CODY: Again, awkward.

There was something undeniably special about the State championship in 2010. Though Seth's death left a gaping hole in the heart of Washington, it was as if the State title run helped everyone feel his presence. Again, it went far beyond sports. Seth would have been so proud.

His tragic death, however, raises a lot of questions about both parenting and life. Why do tragedies occur? How do you explain something so unfathomable to your children? Why is it that a single phone call can shatter your world and change your life?

Questions such as these seemed to come to the forefront of all our minds as our children went through high school. For example, the year before the 2008 State championship, I remember being in Iowa with Lorri and the kids, visiting her parents, when Luke received a phone call about one of his best friends, Justin Smith (who threw him the inbounds pass in the State championship game). We found out that Justin's younger brother had tragically passed away.

Luke and I left Iowa immediately, and Luke spent the next three nights with Justin. In the wake of tragedy, Luke was much more expressive about Justin than Tyler was about Seth. All the way home, Luke was calling his friends and former teammates, trying to arrange a get-together to comfort Justin. Justin's mother still talks about how, over the next week, she would always walk through the living room each morning and see several of Justin's friends sleeping next to him on the floor. She says all she would see were several pairs of feet peeking out from the end of their blankets.

I'm not sure if there is an explanation for such numbing tragedies—I believe it would be arrogant to even try to explain them. There is no explanation. We can exhaust ourselves trying to answer the "Why?" questions of life but perhaps a more tangible answer lies in the "How?" questions of life. How can our sufferings have a redemptive aspect to them? How can we allow God to turn our incomprehensible hurt and pain into a blessing for others? How can these reminders of the frailty of life, these lofty questions lacking answers, allow us to lead lives full of meaning and purpose?

All Lorri and I could do was offer our presence to both our children and the families who were suffering firsthand. There is no use attempting to explain it. It is not the time to say anything along the lines of "God has a plan" or "I know what you are going through." In fact, it is insulting to do so. The response, rather, must lie in presence and availability.

Sometimes, this is the most valuable thing you can offer as a parent or a friend: your presence. This is also what God does for us.

While the Hatchets' State championship run in 2010 was unexpected, Washington natives fully expected one in 2011, so much, in fact, that several fans started calling Lorri in the athletic office to tell her they had reserved suites at Conseco Fieldhouse for the State championship game at the start of the season.

They were right.

The 2011 season, Cody's senior year, featured Washington basketball at its finest. They finished 24-4 on the year, waltzing through the postseason as they defeated each of their opponents by 10 points or more and an average margin of victory of 18.5 points per game. They defeated Culver 61-46 in the State title game to win their third title in four years. Cody became only the fourth player in Indiana basketball history to win three State titles, and Coach Miiller became the ninth coach in Indiana history to win three State titles. ✪

This was great for the town of Washington, but in regard to Cody's antagonistic ways, it was probably the worst thing that could have happened for Tyler and Luke. Once, we were sitting around the dinner table and Cody questioned, "Hey, Luke, how many State titles did you win again?"

CODY: My State championship my senior year gets one paragraph?!? Thanks!!!

"One," Luke grumbled.

"Not bad," Cody replied. "How about you, Tyler?"

"Two," Tyler murmured.

"Not bad," Cody said again.

Cody didn't even need to say anything else.

His mischievous grin said it all: *How's it feel to live in the shadow of your baby brother?*

\WⱮ/

When Washington went to the State championship in 2011, Tom Boyd made another trailer featuring Washington's Mr. Basketball award winners: Steve Bouchie in 1979, Luke in 2005, Tyler in 2008, and Cody, who Washington hoped would win in 2011 (he eventually did)—the first time in the award's seventy-five-year history that three brothers had won it. ✤

In order to include the picture of Luke's reaction to The Shot with Tyler celebrating in the background, Tom had to purchase the rights to the photograph from the *Indianapolis Star*. Again, Tom is one of the most generous, passionate, and dedicated ambassadors for the town of Washington. After each of the State championships, Tom would have the entire town over to his property where the trailers are parked for a giant bonfire and celebration of the championship. He would put on a fireworks show that was bigger than the community's Fourth of July celebration.

In a way, Tom's four trailers perfectly describe our boys' rides with the Hatchets. Luke, Tyler, and Cody may have played good basketball, but it was the people and community that made it special. Tom's

CODY: Since my freshman year of high school, I drove past a sign on my way to school every morning that said, "Welcome to Washington, Home of Mr. Basketball Steve Bouchie, Mr. Basketball Luke Zeller, Mr. Basketball Tyler Zeller." I always wondered if I would be up there.

I understood that the Mr. Basketball award was an individual award available only to seniors, and that I didn't have any control over who voted for me. Part of Mr. Basketball depends on who else is in your class. Still, I wondered if I would ever join my brothers on the sign.

trailers were a gathering place on the streets of Indianapolis each time we made a State championship run. It seemed to represent not only a memory in the basketball realm but also a piece of Washington. There is nothing flashy or showy about a semi-trailer—if anything, it only looks awkward on the streets of a big city—and yet people could see our passion because of its magnitude.

The trailers aren't so much a reminder of the ride our boys had, but more so a reminder of the ride we all shared, as a community, as one, through the highs and the lows. The trailers are a reminder of life and how it's so much easier if we go through it together.

We might have celebrated Coach Omer's first State championship in his Hall of Fame career but we also celebrated the life of his beloved wife. Justin Smith might have wrapped his arms around Luke after making the inbounds pass that led to the buzzer-beater in the State championship, but Luke also slept next to him for days on end when Justin's younger brother passed away. The Hatchet House might have been jam-packed each evening there was a basketball game, but it was also overflowing whenever they held a memorial service for Seth Coy.

Basketball might have brought us all together, but now it's the relationships that live on.

08 THE FOURTH ZELLER SON
by Lorri Zeller

During Luke's senior year of high school, I remember my brother telling me, "If Luke visits Stanford, the campus is so beautiful he will go."

Luke had received numerous offers, which included both Stanford University in Northern California's Bay Area and the University of Notre Dame in northern Indiana. But when my brother said this to me, it all became very real, and I realized something: *My son could be moving 2,300 miles away.*

That's *seven* states. That's *two* time zones. Need I go on? To me, it felt like an entire world away from our homey southern Indiana cornfields.

I would often catch my imagination running wild during this time. After watching every single one of Luke's high school games in person, we'd be forced to watch most of his college games on television if he went to Stanford. After seeing him just about every single day for his entire life, it would most likely be reduced to holidays if he had to travel from California. Then, what about after school? Would he ever return to Indiana long-term again? Or would he love California so much that he'd make it his home? Was I losing my son? Simply sending him off to college was difficult enough, but sending him all the way to *California?* Really? ✵

These were restless nights for me. To be honest, in my deepest long-

LUKE: I feel like Mom has had to relive so many of these emotions while writing these chapters.

ings, I wanted to say something to Luke. I wanted to make a "suggestion" or offer my "opinion" on the situation.

"Luke," I pictured myself saying, "if you want to go to Stanford, that's fine, but your brothers won't be able to watch many of your games. You know how much it means to them to watch your games."

These were my raw thoughts and emotions. Though I knew the situation was out of my control, though I knew Luke could ultimately attend whatever school he liked the most, my desire was to control the situation in any little way I could. This desire is only natural when something arises that involves people you love, but it must be controlled, nonetheless.

As I wrestled with these thoughts, I was reminded of my own college decision. I wanted to attend the University of Missouri. It was where my brother Al went, and he had an amazing experience there. The University of Missouri, however, was four and a half hours south of Springville, Iowa.

It wasn't easy for Mom when Al was away, so when it came time for me to make a college decision, my mom used a black, permanent marker to draw a circle around Springville on a map, covering a ninety-mile radius. "You can go to any college within this circle," she told me.

If you analyze her motives, she drew the circle because she loved me. She didn't want to lose me, just as I didn't want to lose Luke. If she didn't love me, she wouldn't have cared where I went. I've learned that the desire to control is not a bad thing, but acting on it can be.

I ended up playing at Division III Coe College, less than a half hour away from home. And oh, how I wished I could draw a thick, black circle around Washington for Luke!

We scheduled a visit to Stanford and purchased plane tickets from Indianapolis to San Francisco. The plan was to visit Notre Dame one weekend, then visit Stanford the next. After that, we would most likely schedule even more visits. After all, Luke had his selection "narrowed" down to nineteen schools—that's right, *nineteen*. Stanford, however, made me the most nervous.

I never said anything to Luke about how I was feeling. I had made that mistake after his first college visit to the University of Illinois. "Well, what'd you think?" I said as we all got into the car. "What did you like? What did you not like about it?"

Everyone in the car just looked at me.

I was never allowed to ask a question again. I was told I needed to let Luke "digest" each visit. So instead of asking questions, with our visit to Stanford a couple of weeks away, I would cry behind closed doors—seriously—or express myself to Steve in private. ✻

Many times, it felt like I was ignoring the elephant in the room. I would sometimes ask Luke other questions that were less direct like, "How are you feeling about playing college basketball?" or, "Are you excited to visit Stanford?" (I was trying to get answers.) But he would usually respond with something like, "Yeah, it will be fun," or, "Yeah, I'm excited," then change the subject to something, that, in my mind, was incredibly meaningless.

LUKE: Wow, Mom.

TYLER: Doesn't surprise me.

I wanted to talk through it with the people I loved. I wanted someone to throw me a bone every now and then and give me some information. Plus, picking a school is a big decision! I wanted Luke to *express* himself. But all he wanted to do was take a nap. And so did Tyler. And Cody. And even Steve. I sometimes wondered if men thought about anything at all! There were times I wondered if Luke was even planning on *attending* college.

"It's in God's hands," Luke would often times say.

I'd be thinking to myself, "Yeah, but you're the one who has to sign your letter of intent!" ✻

Steve learned throughout the recruiting process, too. At first, he was extremely involved—calling schools on his own and setting up college visits without Luke knowing. But he learned to give Luke

CODY: I remember tagging along on a lot of Luke's recruiting visits. On one of his visits to IU (Coach Mike Davis was recruiting him), I remember A.J. Moye coming up to me and asking, "Hey, little guy, wanna play one-on-one?" A.J. Moye—a hero to

every Hoosier since his game-saving, last-second block that beat No. 1 Duke in IU's 2002 NCAA tournament run! Being the youngest, I was so spoiled.

space, and we started controlling the recruiting process, rather than allowing the process to control us. This became a saying we lived by as each of our boys went through the recruiting process: *Control the process; don't let the process control you.*

Eventually, the weekend rolled around to visit Notre Dame. Steve and Cody were really excited to go up to South Bend because they were huge college football fans. Actually, they were *obsessed* with college football. Whenever Notre Dame first started recruiting Luke, I remember Steve and Cody looking up Notre Dame's football games and trying to get Luke to schedule his recruiting visits around the Irish's biggest matchups. Because of Steve and Cody, we had Notre Dame propaganda all over the house. 🏀

We made the four-and-a-half-hour trip from Washington to South Bend, and I was thinking to myself, "*This* feels like a long way away; I can't even imagine how far away Stanford is."

We arrived at Notre Dame, toured the campus, and spent a lot of time with Notre Dame head coach Mike Brey. Luke loved everything about the school and everything about the basketball program.

CODY: One day, Dad and I were talking about Notre Dame football and Mom got mad at us and said, "You guys are going to sway Luke's decision because all you guys do is talk about Notre Dame!" I think Mom wanted Luke to stay much closer to home.

On the way back down to Washington, I resisted asking questions and simply talked to Steve and Luke about who knows what. Our conversations, to me, felt incredibly forced because I was trying to ignore what I wanted to know the most. Eventually, Luke spoke up from the backseat, out of nowhere.

"That's it," he said.

"What?" I asked.

"That's it," he repeated. "That's where I'm going."

We didn't even fly to California the next weekend. The plane tickets went to waste and we threw more than $1,000 down the drain, but I must admit: I didn't even care.

It might have been four and a half hours away, but at least he was staying in Indiana.

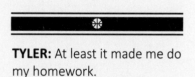

Tyler's college decision received even more media attention than Luke's. Schools were pursuing him with full force. The *Indianapolis Star* even ran a special article in the sports section headlined "Chasing Tyler." But by this time, as Steve says, we were controlling the process; it was not controlling us.

One coach (whom I will not name) called Tyler practically every day, eventually overwhelming him. The coach would talk for at least an hour each time, and Tyler, as quiet as he is, would put the phone on speaker, lie on his bed, and work on his calculus homework, occasionally picking the phone up and saying, "Uh, huh." ⬤

One time, another coach (whom I will not name) and his assistants came over to our house for an official home visit. It was a very formal meeting, and there were at least eight people in our living room: the

---
⬤

TYLER: At least it made me do my homework.

---

coach, his assistant, Coach Miiller, Coach Miiller's wife, Tyler (obviously), Cody, Steve, and me. Luke was at college.

The coach had planned a very thorough presentation with slideshows and game film, detailing exactly how Tyler would fit into their offense and be an immediate contribution to the team. It was impressive. And it was easy to see how thought-out Tyler's absorption into the team had been by the coach and his staff—easily the most detailed presentation any coach had given. But . . . there was one problem.

The entire presentation, the coach kept calling Tyler by the wrong name. Apparently, we had a fourth son named Travis Zeller.

"So, Travis, this is exactly why we need you on our team," the coach would say. His assistant would try to nudge him inconspicuously. "Tyler," he would whisper. "TYLER!"

But I think the coach was so focused on the presentation that he didn't even notice. He had his eyes set on one thing: convincing Travis Zeller he would be a good fit in the program.

After the fourth or fifth time, I leaned over and whispered to Steve, "Is he calling him Travis?" Steve nodded uncomfortably.

It wasn't a deal-breaker for Tyler, but it certainly made the meeting awkward. I actually felt bad for the coach. He had done so much research but botched the most basic of things. It was painful to watch.

Tyler was probably used to things like that. And I don't think it bothered him. Nor do I think he cared. As the middle child and most introverted of all our children, he was often times looked over the most outside of the basketball community. Many outside of Washington didn't know we even had a middle child!

A few years later in San Diego, however, when Tyler was playing college basketball and participated in the inaugural Carrier Classic on an aircraft carrier on Veteran's Day, he had an opportunity to meet President Barack Obama before the game. As the president went down the line and shook all the players' hands, Tyler held out his hand toward the president. "I'm Tyler Zeller," he said.

President Obama playfully nudged him, shaking his hand, "Big Z, you don't have to introduce yourself! I know you." ❁

Maybe the unnamed coach should have hired President Obama as a recruiter.

> **TYLER:** That was actually a really cool moment.

The game on the aircraft carrier, of course, was when Tyler was playing college basketball at the University of North Carolina. And, as you can imagine, sending him ten hours away to Chapel Hill brought up some of the same emotions I had when it looked like Luke might go to Stanford. ❁

This time, however, it was real.

I remember picking Tyler up from the airport after his official visit to the University of North Carolina, and seeing a grin on his face

> **TYLER:** Oh no, here we go again . . .

as he approached me. For someone who was exactly like Steve, showing far less emotion than both Luke and Cody, there was something about Tyler's smile that affirmed everything he had just experienced with head coach Roy Williams and UNC. Somehow, there, in that moment, I knew exactly where he was going to go to school. Seeing this helped me prepare mentally and emotionally to send him off because of the happiness I saw on his face when I picked him up at the airport.

His return home, however, was also a return to an unorthodox amount of Indiana pressure that no eighteen-year-old kid can adequately prepare for. It was as if every part of the state *expected* him to stay in Indiana. He had narrowed his college choices to his "Final Four," which included Notre Dame, Indiana, Purdue, and North Carolina. Many expected him to sign at Notre Dame and play alongside Luke for his senior year. Most expected him to stay close to Washington and join Eric Gordon and D.J. White at Indiana. Then there was head coach Matt Painter at Purdue, who had been recruiting Tyler longer than any other coach in the country. Among those three Indiana schools, most believed he would stay in his home state for college.

There were times, I think, that the pressure in Indiana got to him. Everyone was in his ear telling him a different place to go. A week before his scheduled decision, we had sat in Coach Miiller's office and Tyler said that he wanted to go back and visit every school all over again. We tried to politely tell Tyler that there was nothing else to learn and that he had to trust his instincts. Steve and I could tell he was struggling to pull the trigger on North Carolina.

One day, Tyler was up in his room when Steve decided he was going to help Tyler realize where he wanted to go. It was obvious Tyler had been anxious over his upcoming college decision.

Steve went up the stairs and knocked on Tyler's bedroom door.

"Come in," Tyler said.

Steve entered.

"IU is where you need to go," Steve said boldly. ✪

"What?" Tyler said.

"I've made up my mind," Steve said. "You just need to go to IU."

"But—" Tyler interrupted.

TYLER: It caught me off guard. I've never been one to use a lot of words anyway, so I think it just made me grumpy. I was shocked Dad said something that was so upfront. Mom and Dad hardly ever weighed in on matters like that because they wanted us, as children, to decide for ourselves.

"Listen," Steve said, "if you become Mr. Basketball, it would be a perfect fit. And it will be great for publicity. They'll take care of you locally. You'll become the face of Indiana college hoops. It's your only option that makes sense."

Steve went on and on for several more minutes, naming every single reason why he should go to Indiana and expounding on every argument. Tyler was gradually getting more and more upset and flustered, trying to interject and argue every one of Steve's points. ✺

Eventually, Tyler left his room and came downstairs, as if to escape Steve's opinion. Steve followed him.

"Dad is convinced I need to go to IU," Tyler vented to me.

TYLER: I really was. I didn't understand what had gotten into him.

I didn't respond as Tyler frantically shuffled through the kitchen. He was obviously rattled.

"Well," I eventually smiled, "looks like you've made up your mind."

Tyler looked up at me, then over his shoulder at Steve, who was also smiling. Tyler grinned, suddenly understanding why Steve did what he did.

Truth is, Steve didn't care where Tyler went. Steve wanted *Tyler* to realize which school he wanted to attend.

"Looks like I'm going to North Carolina," he grinned.

The only time Steve "offered his opinion" in our children's college selections was whenever it helped *them* realize what *their* opinion naturally was. We gave them freedom to choose on their own and only offered advice if, one, they asked for it, or, in Tyler's case, it helped free his mind up more.

It wasn't easy to watch him go. But in a sense, it was—because I knew how happy he'd be as a Tar Heel. It was a perfect fit for him.

His grin at the airport, and his smile that day in the kitchen was enough to bring me peace even though he was ten hours away.

None of us were prepared for the media firestorm revolving around Cody's college decision. We thought Luke's was crazy, and we thought Tyler's was crazier, but Cody's gathered more attention than both Luke and Tyler combined.

While working in Washington's athletic department Cody's senior year, I would get calls to our school line from both the local and national media, hoping to interview me and discover *anything* about Cody's upcoming decision.

"What does Cody think about Butler?" they would ask.

"I'm not sure," I would shrug.

"What do you guys talk about at home?" they would ask.

"We don't," I would say.

"You don't talk about it at all?" they may challenge, suspiciously.

"We really don't talk about it," I'd laugh. "I don't know where he's at on it."

Radio personality Dan Dakich, a former Indiana University player, assistant coach, and even interim head coach after Kelvin Sampson's departure, claimed on his Indianapolis radio show that he knew where Cody was going to school from a source. I found it funny because Steve and I didn't even know where Cody was going. *Cody* didn't even know where he was going. Of course, in the end, he said that the "source" he spoke of was himself, Dan Dakich.

My co-workers and friends would ask me some of the same questions, wondering if I was just being ambiguous with the media because, well, it was the media. "I really have no idea," I would tell them. "We really don't talk about it."

This was another thing that was different about Cody. While Luke had an "A-ha! moment" in the car with Steve and me on the way back from Notre Dame and Tyler had his with Steve and me in the kitchen, Cody viewed home as more of a sanctuary.

While his classmates were asking him about it throughout the school day, his teammates were asking him about it at practice after school, and college coaches across the country were calling him in the evenings, being at home with us was a peaceful place for Cody where he *didn't* talk about it. Whereas Luke and Tyler used the confines of our home to process their decisions (though it didn't seem like it because they hardly talked), home and family were strictly an escape for Cody. It was his refuge.

Every once in a while, we would ask him a question about his decision, just to give him the opportunity to open up. But if he dodged the question or wanted to talk about something else, that is what we would do. There was no urgency to keep pushing it. We respected each other, and there was always something else to talk about. Asking your children a question or two can demonstrate that you care. Bombarding them with questions can exhaust them and ultimately demonstrate that you desire to control them.

Once, we went on a college visit with Coach Miiller, and he started asking Cody questions after the visit. Everyone in our family shot Coach Miiller a look as if to say, "You're not allowed to ask those questions. Let him process things."

But this is our natural desire as parents or coaches—to be in the "know."

Every once in a while, Cody would talk to Steve about it, but only whenever the time was right for Cody. In parenting, there is a time for everything—and often times, that timing is decided by your children. This can be a difficult thing, but we believed it was important to give Cody space to process it all on his own. If he needed to talk about it, he would talk to Steve. ✦

In each situation with our children, Steve and I had different

CODY: One of the things I enjoyed most about the recruiting process was going through different college football schedules with Dad and scheduling most of my visits around college football games. My favorites were watching Michigan and Penn State play at the Big House and Ohio State play USC on a Saturday night in Columbus. If I was going up for a recruiting visit, why not see a football game while we were at it? We figured we might as well kill two birds with one stone. I eventually decided that I wanted to go to a basketball school, though I based my recruiting around football.

roles, and we knew these roles. Just as the boys went to Steve for help with their math homework and to me for help with their English homework, they went to Steve for help with their college decisions and to me for help in other areas, such as relationship advice or day-to-day, practical things like mailing a package or running an errand. It didn't matter whom our children confided in as long as they felt comfortable to confide in one of us. We were a team.

A week before Cody was scheduled to make his decision, he opened up to Steve about how he was feeling. It was a Saturday morning, and I was in our bedroom getting ready to start the day while Steve was up talking to Cody. Steve finished talking to Cody, then came into our bedroom.

"Well," Steve said, "he's going to North Carolina."

"Really?" I said, somewhat surprised, and also processing the reality that *another* one of my sons was going to move ten hours away.

"Yep, I'm pretty sure he's going to North Carolina," Steve said again.

I got quiet. Steve did not say anything, knowing I needed to process it all. He told me he was going to the gym to rebound for Cody, and gave me some alone time because he knew I needed it.

When they left, I had the house to myself, and I remember cleaning the house and bawling my eyes out in the process. This was my time to escape—to just vacuum the living room and cry because I was losing my baby!

It was weird to come to grips with the fact that Cody was about to venture off on his own. Though Luke and Tyler had grown up, I always kind of felt like Cody never would. As Kenny Chesney says in his song "Don't Blink," time has a tendency to sneak up on you. Letting go of our final child was hard to understand, though I knew it would happen eventually. It was somewhat of a lonesome feeling—accepting a day I denied would ever come.

It was also hard because it was North Carolina. Cody had narrowed his schools to three primary choices: Indiana University, which was an hour away; Butler University, which was two hours away; and North Carolina, which was *ten* hours away.

I thought Cody might attend Butler because he was closer to Bulldogs head coach Brad Stevens than any other coach. When Butler was recruiting Luke several years before, Stevens was a volunteer assistant, and he and Cody would sneak off during the academic meetings and shoot hoops in Hinkle Fieldhouse. ✹

And I thought he might attend Indiana University because he liked the tradition of Indiana and Assembly Hall. The only negative is that they had fared so poorly in the Big Ten in recent years.

Once, I remember Coach Crean scheduling a meeting with Steve in his office at Assembly Hall and asking him, "What can I do to get through to your son? He doesn't say much when I talk to him."

"Coach," Steve said to him directly, "all you talk about is basketball. Talk to him about something *other* than basketball."

Steve says Coach Crean was diligently taking notes, as if talking about anything other than basketball was completely foreign to him. I think it's a funny scene that shows Coach Crean's determination.

CODY: I've literally been playing "HORSE" with Coach Stevens since I was in fourth grade. When we (the Bobcats, now the Hornets) played the Celtics in 2013 (where Coach Stevens had started coaching), our coaching staff was giving us the scouting report, and I remember thinking, "My own coaching staff spends every day with me and they still don't know me as well as the opposing coach."

Then there was North Carolina. I loved everything about North Carolina except for its geographic location. Tyler was having an incredible experience there, and Roy Williams is one of the greatest coaches of all time. It *did* excite me for Cody and Tyler to play on the same floor again, just like at the Hatchet House, but I was dreading the day I would have to send him off. I knew it would be hard.

What made things especially trying was simply the timing of it all. Luke was overseas playing professional basketball for the Shiga Lakestars in Japan at the time, Tyler was entering his junior year at the University of North Carolina, and Cody was about to join him ten hours away. In those lonely moments, I must admit, I considered moving our entire lives from everything we knew in Indiana to the Carolinas. It felt as if I was losing everything that was a part of me. ✹

By the time Steve and Cody returned from the gym, I had wiped

CODY: To this day, I have no idea why Dad gathered from our conversation that I was going to North Carolina! I never once told him anything about leaning toward UNC. Maybe I said something along the lines of, "It would be neat to play with Tyler again," and he assumed I was heavily considering going down to North Carolina. But, from the very start, I was leaning toward playing at Indiana because of their tradition surrounding the program. So, Dad made Mom cry, not me.

my eyes (and cleaned the entire house). I had my moment, didn't allow Cody to see it, and I was ready to be a mom again and support his college decision, whatever it was. ❁

A few days later, we found out that Steve's prediction was

TYLER: It's really interesting for me to read about this stuff because I didn't know any of this happened. The only time I've ever seen Mom cry is when she dropped me off at college. She forewarned me that this was going to happen, not because she was sad—she was excited about my college decision—but because it was a "Mom thing" or something like that. Mom and Dad did such a good job of not allowing their own emotions to influence our decisions.

wrong, and Cody announced that he would attend Indiana University to help rebuild the basketball program and get an education at one of the top business schools in the country.

The day of his decision, Cody called both Coach Williams and Coach Stevens and told them he was deciding to go to Indiana. ❁

Coach Williams and Coach Stevens were extremely professional about Cody's decision. Coach Williams told him that he was still a part of the family and that he wouldn't treat him or our family any differently than before. Coach

CODY: It was a tough thing to do, but it was the right thing to do. Even when I narrowed my list to three schools, I called all the other schools and told them I wasn't coming. Mom and Dad always felt like it was the respectful thing to do, especially since coaches work so hard to recruit you.

═══════════

Coach Crean.

"I'm going to mess with him," Cody told me, as he hit the "speaker" button on his phone.

Of course he is, I thought to myself.

"Hello," we heard Coach Crean say.

"Hey, Coach Crean," Cody said in a monotone, solemn voice. "I have this press conference this afternoon that I'm heading to, and I feel like—since you've recruited me for so long—that you deserve to hear my decision before the press conference. It's a tough thing to do, but I have to call two coaches and let them know I'm not coming to their school."

Cody paused. ✜

"But the thing is," Cody continued, "I've already made those two calls and told them I am not coming."

Stevens told him that he really enjoyed getting to know him and that he knew he'd be really successful at Indiana.

Next, Cody decided to call

CODY: It was completely silent on the other end.

═══════════

There was a long pause.

Cody and I looked at one another, confused. I guess we expected Coach Crean to say *something* since Cody had ultimately just told him he was coming to IU.

"Hello?" Cody said. "Coach, are you there?"

Nothing.

"Coach? Are you there?"

"Yeah, yeah, yeah," Coach Crean said excitedly, trying to gain his composure. He seemed speechless. Honestly, it sounded like he was crying. ✜

"I'm just so excited!" Coach Crean exclaimed. "You're going to get so much better while you are here! We are so humbled! We're so excited!" ✜

Needless to say, from a personal

═══════════

CODY: We heard a couple sniffles, and Mom and I looked at each other and said, "Is he crying?"

═══════════

CODY: Before the call ended, Coach Crean said, "The next time I cry in front of you will be when we win a national championship."

standpoint, I was happy my baby boy wasn't going ten hours away. But the whole experience was a good exercise for me, nonetheless. I had come face-to-face with the reality of North Carolina, and I can honestly say I was on board with it. I had accepted it. I was even excited for it.

Of course, I was even more excited that my youngest son wasn't going very far from home.

Home must be a safe haven for your children to express themselves. This is what it became to Cody. If your children don't decompress at home, then they'll do it through something else.

We did not figure it out immediately, however. Poor Luke was always the guinea pig. It's a miracle he's even halfway sane today. ✹

There were many car rides where I bombarded Luke with questions and overwhelmed him. There were times I offered my opinion when I should have remained silent, and there were times I tried to control the situation though I needed to give him freedom to come to a

TYLER: Hey, who said that he was sane?

conclusion on his own—even if it was Stanford on the West Coast.

But we learned as we went, while, at the same time, we were not ashamed to step back and analyze our own actions and consider the questions: What can we do to handle this in a better way? How can we serve one another better in our marriage? And how can we serve our children better as parents?

It was more difficult for me to let go of our children than it was for Steve, so Steve helped me by taking interest in what I was feeling. To Steve, our boys were simply going off to school because that was the way life worked. (His simplicity is so complex to me that I'll never understand it.)

But to me, I was letting go. And, though Steve did not necessarily understand what I was feeling, he handled my heart carefully and allowed me to express myself so that I didn't take my stress and emotions out on our children. If I would have broken down and cried in front of Cody when Steve told me he was going to North Carolina, this would have most likely made Cody feel like he needed to put guards up. His home no longer would have felt safe.

But Steve's attention to being a husband allowed me to continue being a mother. His attention toward *our* relationship kept us on the same page and ultimately resulted in creating a home that felt safe and freeing for our children, rather than stressful and restricting. Again, in our household, many parenting issues could be boiled down to my relationship with Steve. The more we focused on our relationship with each other, the healthier the environment was for our children. This creates freedom. This creates safety.

A healthy husband-and-wife relationship creates this environment, but so does the proper mindset in regard to *partnering* with your children and making their passions flourish rather than *controlling* them to fit into your own plans. Naturally, I wanted to control Luke or influence him to attend a school that would be convenient for *me* and all that I was feeling. But I had to train myself (with Steve's help) to come alongside Luke, regardless of how far away he went, and give him the freedom and confidence that allowed him to be successful. ✹

We wanted to put our children in the best position to make a decision and excel. It's common to approach decisions too systematically and say something along the lines of, "We're going to send Tyler to North Carolina because they've had 'X' number of people make it to the NBA." However, no formula can contain God's plan for our lives. And we didn't want any of our boys to look back on their college basketball careers and say, "Mom and

LUKE: This is another one of Mom and Dad's parenting concepts that remind me a lot of our relationship with God. God does not control us as if we are puppets. Instead, He has given each one of us a unique set of talents, passions, and desires, and He wants to partner with us. He has given us the freedom to pursue things that align with our gifts and bring glory to Him, and he wants to bring them to life. In His love, there is freedom. His will is not to control but rather to enable. He wants to unleash us into the world. In His grace, he puts His arm around us and says to us, "Son, Daughter, where would you like to go? Let's go there together."

Dad made me go here." It had to be *their* decision, even if our chief (even natural) desire was to make that decision for them.

In freedom, there is safety. And this was the goal for our home, for it to be free and safe. Even if I had to cry while vacuuming behind closed doors.

Our engagement picture. (1985)

⇑ *Basketball on Steve's farm growing up.*

⇓ *Tyler was only a baby; but apparently wrestling started ear in our household. (1990)*

⇑ *Basketball on Lorri's farm growing up.*

⇑ One of our favorite photos of the boys. It describes their personalities perfectly. Luke is loving and caring; Tyler is annoyed by little Cody; and Cody, well...he's just the baby.

⇓ Luke (7), Tyler (4), and Cody (1).

⇑ Not a fun Easter for the Zeller children.
All of them contracted chickenpox. (1993)

⇐ We never expected basketball to be such a big part of our lives; but it's funny now to look back on a picture like this. (March 1995)

⇑ Cody wearing Steve's basketball clothes. (February 1994)

⇑ Moving to Indiana. Cody and Tyler don't seem too happy about it. (July 1993)

⟵ Cody's Heisman pose. (August 2002)

⇑ John Wooden at the McDonald's All-American games. Cody blocked the sun for him so he could sign books. (Spring 2005)

⇑ Even comparing heights was a competition. Cody wins in this picture. (2006)

⇑ *The McDonald's All-American game. They estimated sizes for them, so Luke's warm-ups were HUGE! (2005)*

⇑ *Luke's senior year along with a childhood picture when he was eighteen months old that mirrors this pose. (December 2004)*

⇑ Dave Omer and his wife Wilda on the medal stand at State. Wilda, who was battling cancer, passed away a few months later. (State 2005)

⇓ Luke during his senior year in high school.

Tyler as a senior in high school. (January 2008)

Tyler, Indiana Mr. Basketball. (June 2008) ⇒

⇑ Semi-trailer for Tyler's State tournament year. (March 2008)

⇑ Tyler and Seth Coy after a tournament win in March 2008. (Seth was killed in a car accident during his freshman year of college.)

⇐ *Cody during his freshman year of high school. (January 2008)*

⇑ *Cody with his State championship medal, shown with his high school coach, Gene Miiller and his college coach, Tom Crean. (2011)*

⇐ *Semi-trailer for Cody's State tournament year. (March 2011)*

We purchased a brick for each of our boys at the Indiana Basketball ⇑
Hall of Fame to commemorate their Mr. Basketball awards.

Cody with one of his State championship trophies. (March 2010)

Christmas Eve 2008. Tyler had a left broken wrist; Cody had a left broken finger; and Luke would injure his left thumb the following week!

⇑ *Three boys with their grandpa, Marvin Eberhard (Lorri's dad). Marvin won the 19 State championship in Nebraska, while wearing No. 40. Each of our boys wore No. in his honor. (2007)*

Luke as a freshman at Notre Dame.
(February 2006)

University of Notre Dame

Mike Dickbernd/ Indiana University

Cody as a freshman at Indiana.
(November 2011)

Jeffrey Camarati/UNC Sports

⇐ Tyler at North Carolina.

⇑ With both Luke (Notre Dame) and Tyler (UN
in the Maui Invitational, we wore split shir
to support both of them. (November 2008

⇑ We did the same thing during the Big 10/ACC Challenge. Cody (IU) was a freshman
they played N.C. State. We then traveled to Chapel Hill where we watched Tyler (UNC,
a senior play Wisconsin. Two games on the same night....and two wins! (November 2C

⇐ Luke's graduation from Notre Dame.
(May 2009)

⇑ Luke being honored at Notre Dame Senior
Night. (2009)

⇑ The UNC vs. Michigan State game at the First Carrier Classic with Luke's wife,
Hope. President Obama shook Tyler's hand before the game and called him "Big Z".
(November 2011)

← Tyler's graduation from UNC. (2012)

Cody and IU coach Tom Crean. ⟹

Jeffrey Camarati/UNC Sports

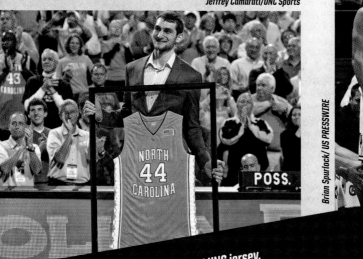

Brian Spurlock/ US PRESSWIRE

⇧ Tyler holding his retired UNC jersey.

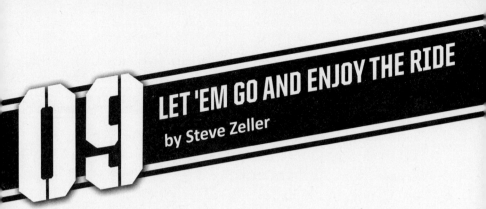
There's an egg, potato, coffee grounds, and a pot of boiling water. The egg is soft on the inside, but if you put it in boiling water, it will become hard. The potato is hard or tough on the inside, but in the boiling water, it becomes soft, sometimes mushy. The coffee grounds change into something completely different—coffee—when they are added to boiling water.

Each object reacts differently in the pot of boiling water, and each one of our boys acted differently in the face of adversity.

The only difference in this phase of their lives—as they left our home and journeyed through college—was that it was no longer our job to carry them through the fire. They were on their own. And each situation presented its own set of challenges and opportunities for us to learn and also adjust as parents.

ᴠᴠᴠᴠᴠᴠ

Trusting the Authority

Luke enjoyed his freshman year at Notre Dame in 2005. He played in twenty-seven of the Fighting Irish's games, made nine starts, and learned a lot about what it took to play at the college level. It might have been a bit humbling for him to go from being a McDonald's All-American and Indiana Mr. Basketball his senior year at Washington to averaging 3.4 points and 3.1 rebounds per game at Notre Dame, but, in many ways, it was just like the McDonald's All-American game his senior year—on the national level, he was just another player. ✹

He was once again at the bottom of the totem pole, but he was once again determined to succeed, just as he had done in high school. He was ready to help put Notre Dame on the map, just as he had helped put Washington on the map. And he was ready to put himself in a good position to play at the next

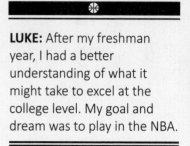

LUKE: After my freshman year, I had a better understanding of what it might take to excel at the college level. My goal and dream was to play in the NBA.

level professionally, just as he had put himself in a good position to play at the next level collegiately.

His freshman year, his coaches challenged him to get bigger and stronger and work his way up to 250 pounds. He had worked hard and done so. His offseason heading into his sophomore year, his coaches challenged him to get in really good shape because they expected him to play thirty minutes a game. He worked harder than ever and entered his sophomore season in the best shape of his life.

In the first pre-season game of his sophomore season, however, he got only six minutes of playing time. For Luke, this was a huge blow. He realized that his role on the team might not end up being what he hoped, what he had worked so hard for, and what he had been told. He began having doubts about his decision to attend Notre Dame, and the period following that first pre-season game became the lowest moment of his college career. Nothing was turning out the way he had planned, and it made him think about a lot of things.

It was a defining moment in his frustration, but it also became a defining moment in his commitment to Notre Dame. After the pre-season game, he called one of his high school teammates who was playing for Brad Stevens at Butler.

"You could transfer and come to Butler to play for Coach Stevens," his friend told him.

"I don't know," Luke eventually said, "things aren't going well here, but I still want to be a Notre Dame guy. I'm loyal to Notre Dame."

As the season continued, Luke's playing time woes also continued. He got some starts at the beginning of the season, but was soon replaced by a talented, freshman post player by the name of Luke Harangody.

Harangody proved to be a special pickup for the Irish, as he went on to average 11.2 points per game and 6.2 rebounds per game, earning Big East All-Rookie First Team honors. Luke struggled to find his place and role on the team as the season ensued, and his playing time dwindled more and more.

Later in the season, Luke received a glimpse of hope and was told that he was going to start alongside Harangody in one of Notre Dame's Big East contests. Luke relayed the information to us, so we decided to make the five-hour drive and take a family trip up to Notre Dame. Lorri and I both took half a day off of work. We were excited.

Luke, however, didn't start. He didn't even get to play until about two minutes left in the game, when he was finally substituted onto the floor. I don't even remember who Notre Dame played that night, but Lorri later dubbed it "The Worst Road Trip Ever." We got back to Washington at three in the morning, and Lorri and I were both at work in a few hours.

LUKE: I didn't play much, but it meant a lot to me that Mom and Dad came. One thing I really appreciated about them during this time was that they supported me more than they supported the goal. My goal that night might have been to be in the starting lineup and play thirty minutes, but their support of me came first. That made all the difference in the world. Their support of me was not performance-based. It's also what God does for us. If His love was performance-based, we would always fall short.

Luke's struggles at Notre Dame forced us to answer some difficult questions.

What should our role be as parents when our child is going through a rough time? Especially when the source of our frustration had to do with the decisions being made about our son's playing time?

Lorri and I are old school in this regard, but we never felt like it was appropriate to talk to our children's college coaches regarding playing time or the way they ran their program. To me, the overly involved approach that parents take in their relationships with coaches, even at the college level, is inappropriate and controlling. Luke was my son. Of course I was going to take Luke's side, believing he deserved more playing time. Of course I was going to want what was best for Luke. Of course it pained us to see Luke struggling. But part of being a parent is allowing coaches to be coaches.

When Luke was going through the recruiting process, I remembered former Purdue head coach Gene Keady mentioning that he would get frustrated with parents who questioned the head coach on a collegiate level. I believe Coach Keady had a reason to be frustrated. Even if I felt like my son *should* be receiving more playing time at Notre Dame, it didn't matter—I wasn't the coach.

As parents, it's important to know both your own role and the roles of others in the lives of your children. Attempting to play every role in your children's lives is a form of coddling and ultimately reflects your desire to control every situation, thus stunting their own maturation.

When it came to Notre Dame's basketball team, the coaching staff had the authority. Scripture is very clear that Christians should always submit to those who are above them in authority—whether it's a parent, a coach, a boss, or member of law enforcement. It was in the coaching staff's authority to play Luke or not play Luke, however they saw fit.

When our children received college scholarships to play basketball, Lorri and I both treated it as if our children were employed by the school. In a way, they were. At that point, they belonged to the university and were under the authority of their coaches, professors, and advisors. It would be absurd (and also rather embarrassing) for Luke if he held an office job and I was continually calling the owner of the company, bugging him to give Luke a raise. Why? Because, at that point, he belongs to his boss. He has an employer. I'm not his employer. I'm his parent.

Lorri and I might be going somewhat against the grain in a day and age where it's normal for parents to be heavily involved and in constant communication with their children's coaches, even college coaches, but I believe our society needs more of a "let them go" mentality.

It's difficult for parents to sit on the sidelines and allow the game to unfold. It was just as difficult for us. But this was also part of letting go. This was part of moving from discipline to freedom, from parenthood to friendship, and part of our sons' moving from boyhood to manhood.

Luke's final season (and his college career, in general) didn't turn out as he had envisioned, but he allowed the adversity to make him both a better person and player. He decided early on, that, despite how poorly basketball was shaping up for him, he would, one, stay at Notre Dame and fulfill the four-year commitment he made to Coach Brey as a freshman, and, two, continue to pursue his dream of playing in the NBA. He allowed his sub-par college career to add to his journey and make for a greater story. His on-the-floor struggles brought him closer to God and forced him to depend on God more.

Luke will tell you that his lack of playing time at Notre Dame made him work that much harder, which ultimately prepared him to work hard in his unorthodox journey in professional basketball. Notre Dame made him mature quicker in the basketball sphere. It helped him awaken to the reality that it's never easy, that achieving our dreams has mountains along the way that must be climbed.

And, though his college career might not have been what he had envisioned, I don't want it to sound like it was void of highlights. He still had some exciting games and became somewhat of a three-point specialist for the Irish. One game his senior season, he matched his career-high with 18 points against No. 3 Pittsburgh . . . all in the first half . . . all on three-pointers. On his career, he shot 36 percent from the three-point line and hit 107 threes—a much different role than both Tyler and Cody would end up playing in college.

At Notre Dame, he also found joy in other areas of life beyond the hardwood. He began thinking more about how he might be able to use his entrepreneurship degree and once again revisited the hypothetical basketball camp he had dreamt up on our drives from Washington to his AAU tournaments in Fort Wayne. He took great pride in Notre Dame's business school, which is consistently rated one of the best in the country. Today, as Luke reflects, he knows that Notre Dame prepared him well for some of his other business endeavors in life, like his basketball ministry, DistinXion. 🏀

He also had an incredible social experience and made some lifelong friends in South Bend. Adding to that, he met his future wife there in northern Indiana: a young woman named Hope Grame, who was attending Bethel College in Mishawaka, on the outskirts of South Bend.

LUKE: God had a much bigger plan than anything that was a struggle at Notre Dame. If I could have gone straight to the NBA after college, then DistinXion probably wouldn't have come about until much later in my life, or it might not have happened at all.

Overall, letting him go and allowing him to go through the process on his own, rather than hovering over his basketball career like hungry vultures, allowed him to grow even more. He left Washington as a boy, and he graduated from Notre Dame as a man, ready to be unleashed into the world.

Good ultimately came from the struggle. He discovered joy in other areas of life, passions in other areas of life, and used the resistance in his basketball career to motivate him even more on the basketball floor.

Trusting Your Parenting

Soon, Tyler was thrown into the boiling water, as well.

Tyler began his freshman year at North Carolina, starting in place of reigning National Player of the Year Tyler Hansbrough, who was nursing an injured shin at the time. The season opener against Pennsylvania was on a Saturday, so Cody and I decided to fly to Chapel Hill, watch the game, and fly back the same day.

Lorri stayed at home because her father had undergone surgery the week before, and she had spent four days in Iowa with him. She felt like she needed to get caught up on things around the house. Plus, we'd be flying to Hawaii the following week to watch both Notre Dame and North Carolina play in the three-day Maui Invitational; we would have plenty of time to watch both Luke (in his senior year) and Tyler (in his freshman year) play there. Her decision to stay home, however, would be one she would deeply regret in the coming weeks.

North Carolina's opener ended up being a great game to attend as Tyler started his college career off with a bang. He led the team with 18 points as North Carolina coasted to an 86-71 victory. He looked just as dominant at the collegiate level as he did his senior year of high school at Washington.

On Tuesday, North Carolina faced Kentucky for a televised game in Chapel Hill. We chose to tune in and watch the game from Washington since it was in the middle of the workweek. Tyler once again started in the absence of Hansbrough.

Late in the game, however, there was a big-time scare when Tyler attempted a dunk in transition and took a hard foul from Kentucky's Ramon Harris. Tyler took a while to get up, and I immediately knew it was serious.

In our household, we called it the "Three-Second Rule": If any of our boys didn't get up within three seconds after a fall, we knew they might be seriously hurt. Usually, they hopped right back up. Throughout Tyler's high school career, he always seemed to rise to his feet within three seconds, and he never encountered any type of serious injury.

Even when he was younger, I recall a time when Tyler hurt his wrist while playing flag football in third grade. I told him to tape it up and go back into the game. ✵

Following his flag football game, I knew he had hurt his wrist, but I didn't think it was anything serious. Plus, Tyler didn't say anything else about it—for a week. I suppose I should have checked up on him. But I didn't.

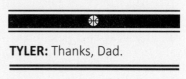

TYLER: Thanks, Dad.

One day, I noticed that, while the boys were swinging on the swing set at the playground and leaping off in mid-air, Tyler was only using one hand to break his fall.

"Tyler," I said, "why don't you use both of your hands?"

"Because my wrist hurts," he told me.

Lorri took him to the doctor, and it turned out he had broken his wrist in two places during the flag football game more than a week before. I felt like the worst parent ever when the doctor asked Lorri when he broke it. He seemed both shocked that any child could deal with the pain for as long as he did and disturbed that his parents could be any less observant.

But that's how I knew his injury in the Kentucky game was bad. Tyler rarely showed any emotion at all, even from the time he was in grade school, especially anything that had to do with weakness.

ESPN went "live" to Erin Andrews in the tunnel for her report, as Tyler walked past her straight to the locker room. "I've seen a lot of football injuries before," she said, "and I can tell just by the looks of this one that it's pretty bad."

As Lorri and I watched everything unfold on the television set from Washington, we began discussing our action plan. Lorri wanted to drive down immediately. She wanted to hop in the car and go. The problem, unfortunately, was that Chapel Hill was ten hours away and the team was flying to Santa Barbara, California, in two days. Then, after their game against UC Santa Barbara, they'd be flying to Hawaii for the Maui Invitational. It wouldn't make sense to drive to North Carolina, hardly be able to see Tyler, then drive back to Indiana to catch our flight to Maui out of Indianapolis. Time alone put us in a difficult scenario. There was nothing to do but wait—parent from afar until we saw him face-to-face in Maui. To Lorri, this felt more like the two years than two days.

My heart hurt for Tyler but I also knew that injuries were part of the game. Lorri, on the other hand, felt very anxious and upset. She felt absolutely helpless.

I had to work the next morning so I went to bed, only to be awakened by the Tar Heels' doctor calling me on my cell phone. He told me Tyler's wrist was most likely broken and that he would probably need surgery.

"Well," I said, "tell Tyler that I said to tape it up so he can go back in."

It was a joke, and I figured it might make Tyler chuckle, considering what happened when he was in grade school playing flag football. There was nothing else I could do, so I didn't see the point of over-reacting to it.

There was a long pause on the other end of the phone.

"Mr. Zeller," the doctor said, "you realize the game is over, right?"

"Yeah, yeah," I said, "it was only a joke. Just tell Tyler I said to tape it up and go back in."

He hesitated. "Okay," he said uncomfortably. "Have a good night, Mr. Zeller." ✸

TYLER: The doctor delivered Dad's message. I laughed and understood Dad was trying to lighten the moment.

But then my doctor asked me, "Does your mom have a cell phone I can call?"

Lorri was up all night, as North Carolina did a great job of calling her and keeping her informed about the details of his wrist injury. She couldn't sleep and was doing all she could to help. Luke was already struggling in his senior season at Notre Dame, and now Tyler was struggling in his freshman season at North Carolina. Needless to say, the start of the 2008-09 season was a tough one for the Zeller family on the hardwood.

The circumstances—being bound to Washington and forced to wait until Maui to see Tyler—made her feel as if she were in a strait-jacket. In many ways for both of us, our plight felt very similar to the playing problems Luke was having at Notre Dame. In either case, there was nothing we could do to help, other than let them venture through the storms as men.

By the next morning, more details regarding Tyler's injury had been revealed to us. The doctor I spoke to had estimated that he'd be out eight weeks; a hand specialist they had brought in believed it might be twelve to sixteen weeks; and by the time he went into surgery late that morning, the surgeon had told us it could be season-ending and possibly career-ending. All of this was taking place while we were ten hours away. Talk about feeling helpless. ✸

Coach Roy Williams called us that day and told us that he had

CODY: Funny side note: All three of us brothers had broken hands/wrists in our Christmas picture that year.

gone into the examining room the night before hoping to comfort Tyler. He had opened the door, seen Tyler sitting on his bed with his head down, and said to him, "You gonna be okay, Big Guy?"

The only light in the room was a dim lamp next to Tyler's hospital bed. When Tyler looked up, Coach Williams said Tyler had a single "alligator tear" streaming down his face. ✻

The story broke Lorri's heart; and before long, she had tears streaming down her face, as well. I, myself, was surprised Tyler even knew how to shed a tear. I admit: I, too, felt helpless.

CODY: Hahahahahahahaha-hahahahahaha!!! Tyler was crying!!!

What made Lorri feel even worse, especially in finding out that his injury could be season-ending or career-ending, was the fact that she hadn't gone with Cody and me to watch North Carolina play Penn in North Carolina's season opener the previous weekend. I told her there was nothing she could do, that she had a lot on her plate, but I understood where she was coming from. Suddenly, we both realized how crucial it was to seize each moment and support our children in their passions whenever we possibly could—no matter how busy we were.

🌾

Another thing we learned in our helpless state was a rather invaluable lesson: We had to trust in our own parenting.

Tyler was a man now—perhaps only a freshman, but a man. He had spent the summer heading into his freshman year away from Washington for the first time, and he *chose* to go to North Carolina. He was on his own, no longer under the roof of our house or under the careful watch of his parents. It was up to him to make his own decisions. It was up to him to listen to the doctors and hand specialists and decide what the best plan of action was. It was up to him to depend on the people around him and to ask for help whenever he needed it. He could call us and we could do our best to comfort him from afar, but he couldn't fully depend on us because we were four states away. He was an adult and we had to trust that we had prepared him adequately to be released into this world. Isn't this one of the purposes of parenthood? To prepare your children to be on their own? Forever treating them as children eliminates one of the primary opportunities of parenting.

We also had to trust in a higher authority. We had to believe God had led Tyler or partnered with Tyler in his decision to attend North Carolina, though it was far away, and therefore we had to trust that— far away from us—God would surround Tyler with the right people to take care of him. The right doctor. The right specialist. The right surgeon. The right people to get him to the airport when his team had already flown out west. Both the big things and the little things. Truly believing in God's sovereignty frees you from the stress associated with micromanagement.

A few days after the initial injury, we finally had the opportunity to be with Tyler once we landed in Maui. To Lorri, the entire experience probably felt like his childbirth all over again. The delay. The loss of control. The feeling that all she wanted to do was be with him but couldn't.

By the time we were finally with him, Tyler was back to his happy-go-lucky self. His surgery had gone well, and his entire arm, up to his bicep, was in a cast and heavily wrapped. ✺

He wasn't allowed to get his arm wet, so when he needed a shower, a UNC manager would come in his room and wrap his entire arm in plastic to protect the bandages. Tyler had accepted the fact that his left wrist was broken, and he had

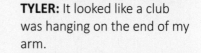

TYLER: It looked like a club was hanging on the end of my arm.

decided he was going to get stronger. He was going to find something redemptive in his present sufferings and use it to his advantage.

Tyler came through the situation with flying colors. His injury, really, was one of the first things he had to go through on his own (without his family on a day-to-day basis) that he hadn't planned for.

He went to North Carolina on his own, but he had planned for that. Nothing, however, could have prepared him for having a potentially career-ending injury. ✳

That weekend in Hawaii, UNC ended up playing Notre Dame in the championship game of the Maui Invitational. It was expected to be the first time ever that the country would witness a Zeller vs. Zeller matchup—something that Lorri always dreaded (I think she was afraid the boys might kill one another if they ever went head-to-head). ✳

When the boys were growing up, they seemed to spend every spare moment playing against each other in something basketball-related. This usually ended with one of them getting ticked off and having a tale to tell Lorri. It became very competitive in just about everything—whether it was a game of "HORSE," playing two-on-two (I was usually on Cody's team) after supper, or shooting on a Nerf hoop inside the house. As they got into high school, we would spend hours upon hours playing in the Hatchet House, where their skills really developed. Cody benefited most from these scrimmages because he was always playing against someone that was older and better than him. ✳

The opportunity for a Zeller vs. Zeller matchup, of course, was thrown out the window the second Tyler injured his wrist in Chapel Hill a few days before. After the game, as the two teams lined up and shook one another's hands, Luke grabbed Tyler and gave him a

TYLER: During this time, a member of the media asked me, "What happens if this becomes a career-ending injury?"

I replied, "Well, I'll be successful at something other than basketball."

LUKE: I think that's a legitimate concern.

CODY: When I was really young, I used to shoot around on a Nerf hoop in the sunroom for hours. Tyler would come in and just stand by the rim and block everything. I would get so mad at him!

big hug. As parents, it was a "Kodak moment."

For Lorri and me, we felt Luke's time at Notre Dame combined with Tyler's injury while he was ten hours away in Chapel Hill taught us a lot about letting go. It was up to them to take everything we had taught them (we hoped it was enough) into the world and handle adversity on their own. *Our roles had changed.* They were on their own, and now, we got to enjoy watching them fly, even if it was through a storm.

Of course, Tyler's injury might have been the most serious of his career up to that point, but it wasn't career-ending. He was out for ten and a half weeks—and he actually was back playing by the final portion of the season. Nonetheless, it was a wake-up call for both of us to never take any moment for granted.

Like Luke's struggles, Tyler will tell you that a lot of good came from the injury. At the start of the 2008-09 season, he was a skinny freshman. But his inability to practice left him with only one option if he wanted to hone his skills: go to the weight room. Over the next several weeks, he put on several pounds of muscle and developed a great relationship with the weight room strength and conditioning coach.

> **TYLER:** My injury actually made me a better basketball player because it made me get stronger quicker.

There was nothing else for him to do but lift and lift and lift. UNC took great care of him throughout the process and taught him a number of exercises he could do with his injury including a one-armed bench press. A loss of control can actually become something that propels us to the next level if we approach hardship with the right attitude. This was true for our children, but also true for us, as parents.

Tyler ended up returning for the final third of the season and playing in about fifteen games that year. After winning a State championship with Washington the year before, his North Carolina team went on to finish the regular season with a 34-4 overall record and a 13-3 conference record in winning the regular-season ACC title. The Tar Heels marched through the NCAA tournament all the way to the Final Four in Detroit. They defeated Villanova 83-69 in the semifinal game to advance to the national championship game against Michigan State.

Since Luke's senior season and career at Notre Dame had come to an end, he and Hope were able to join Lorri, Cody, and me at the national championship game in Detroit at Ford Field. Luke wore a baby blue North Carolina shirt that had "44" and "Zeller" printed on the back.

About fifteen minutes before tip-off, Luke went to the concession stand to get a hot dog for the game. Several "fans" approached Luke while he was in line getting a hot dog and said to him, "Good luck tonight, man." (When you're six foot eleven, it's difficult to blend in.)

Luke enjoyed the opportunity to have some fun.

"Thank you," he'd say. "Hopefully we can get a win. Excuse me while I eat this—I have to make sure I get back to the court before tip-off."

North Carolina ran right over Michigan State, defeating the Spartans 89-72 to win the Tar Heels' fifth national championship—a perfect way for Tyler to start his college career, especially after a scary beginning to the season.

Their national championship was the biggest accomplishment of his college career from a team standpoint. They lost in the championship game of the National Invitation Tournament Tyler's sophomore year, advanced to the Elite Eight before falling to Kentucky during Tyler's junior year, and again fell in the Elite Eight against Kansas during Tyler's senior year.

On a personal level, Tyler's senior season was unlike any other, both because of its mountaintops but also because of its valleys. One of the most trying times of the season came against Duke at the Dean Dome in February.

First off, the Duke/UNC rivalry is one of the fiercest in the nation, and North Carolinians treat each matchup like a national holiday. It's unique in the sense that the universities are located approximately ten miles apart off Tobacco Road, and UNC is a public university while Duke is private. Polls grade the match-up as not just one of the best rivalries in college basketball but one of the best in all of North America. The state of North Carolina might as well shut down whenever the two teams play.

On this particular day, Tyler had a great game going and was continuing to put up a good case for ACC Player of the Year. He scored 19 points and grabbed 8 rebounds in the first half and was dominating the game. He finished with a double-double—23 points and 11 rebounds—but that's not what he'll forever be remembered for in that game.

Duke trailed 84-82 in the late seconds of the game when the Blue Devils' Austin Rivers took the ball up and came off of a screen set by his teammate Mason Plumlee. Tyler switched and tried to put a hand in Rivers' face as he hit a buzzer-beater three-pointer from the right wing. Tyler and the Tar Heels were humiliated. On their home floor. By their biggest rival.

It was the lowest moment of Tyler's college career since his injury—by far. Whatever joy we might have felt whenever Luke hit "The Shot" in the State championship game, this moment had the exact opposite effect. Until the final seconds, he had played a great game, but not being able to defend Rivers' shot was what he would be remembered for. Luke's shot was one of the best in Indiana basketball State championship history; Rivers' was one of the best in the history of the Duke/UNC rivalry.

We didn't realize the magnitude of it all until we walked out of the Dean Dome and saw "WE LOVE YOU TYLER ZELLER" in block letters written on the sidewalk in chalk. Tar Heel Nation was coming alongside him and supporting him, which was cool to see, but he was getting absolutely massacred by Duke fans and some of the media. The next day, many of the pundits pointed out how Tyler shouldn't have switched on the screen or should have been guarding Rivers more tightly. The next day, the front page of *The Daily Tar Heel*, North Carolina's student newspaper, read "BROKEN HEARTED" in huge, bold text next to a picture of Tyler. ❀

When North Carolina went to Duke's Cameron Indoor Stadium a month later, Tyler and the rest of the Tar Heel team were on a mission. It seemed like Austin Rivers' shot was all anyone could talk about for four straight weeks, and the Cameron Crazies had a life-size cutout of Tyler in their student section—wearing a Duke jersey. ❀

Tyler told us that he noticed and heard a few things during warm-ups, but once the game began, he entered his "Tyler Zone." Contrary to what you'd think, Duke fans may have been passionate and brutal during the game, but they also had a deep respect and admiration for those associated with the game, even their opponents. One time, when we were walking to the entrance of Cameron Indoor, a Duke student boisterously pointed out, "Hey, that's Zeller's parents!" Everyone around him, mostly Duke fans, grew silent and didn't harass us at all. They cleared the way for us and allowed us to walk through on the sidewalk.

This particular game, UNC embarrassed Duke on their home

TYLER: I didn't leave my apartment for the next two days because I didn't really want to see anyone. But it actually wasn't the shot that upset me the most. I played the shot wrong and should have been playing higher, but if you look back, I also went two for four on free throws down the stretch. I always prided myself on hitting free throws at the end of the game. If I would have made those two free throws, that would have changed the whole dynamic of the game. I felt like I had let my team down. I had a chance to win it for them.

TYLER: Bleh.

floor, running away with an 88-70 victory to win the ACC regular-season title again. Tyler had 19 points on 9-of-11 shooting and grabbed 10 rebounds. The front page of the sports section in Raleigh's *News & Observer* the following day read "PAYBACK." ✸

Three days later, Tyler was named ACC Player of the Year. He ended up averaging 16.3 points and 9.6 rebounds per game, with 14 double-doubles on the season.

One day, I asked him, "Doesn't that mean that they hang your jersey in the rafters?"

"Yeah," he told me, "I think it does." ✸

His junior and senior seasons, he also received NCAA Academic All-America honors, but his senior season, he was ranked No. 1 out of the five players who received the nationwide award. Lorri and I remember reading his quote in North Carolina's press release. Tyler began by saying: "This is a great honor and something I have worked for my entire four years at Carolina. To be the first Tar Heel to win this award at a school with so much tradition and prestige adds to the honor."

At the start, it sounded like what a typical athlete might say about his accomplishments. But then we

---

TYLER: That game was the quietest I've ever heard Cameron Indoor. Toward the end of the game, one of my teammates said a joke on the floor that Coach Williams heard from the sideline. My teammate got in trouble later. But that's how quiet it was. You could have heard a pin drop. It was almost eerie how silent it was.

TYLER: What meant most to me about the award was the fact that Dad thought it was cool my jersey would hang in the rafters among other North Carolina greats like Michael Jordan. I could tell that he thought that was neat.

---

continued reading: "It truly means a lot to my family. My parents brought me up with the belief that academics are more important than athletics, so as much as it means to me, it may mean even more to my mom and dad. And I thank them for the guidance and support they've always given my brothers and me."

One of the most rewarding things you can experience as a parent is when your children look back and recognize the values in which they were raised.

Trusting the Journey

Tyler's senior year, the 2011-12 season, was an exciting one for the Zeller family. Not only were things going well for him at North Carolina, but it was also Cody's first season at Indiana University.

The hype swirling around Indiana basketball and Cody's arrival in Bloomington was something we never could have fathomed. But, just as we saw Luke deal with his lack of playing time at Notre Dame maturely and Tyler emerge from his wrist injury as a better person and player, we also saw Cody handle the hype and expectations the best way he possibly could have handled it, especially as an eighteen-year-old young man.

After former Hoosier head coach Kelvin Sampson's NCAA indiscretions left the program in shambles in 2007, Indiana had experienced some of its darkest seasons in its esteemed history. Coach Tom Crean tried to clean up the program and the mess he inherited, but his first three seasons were especially trying because of the sanctions that had been placed on the program.

6-25 in 2008; 1-17 in the Big Ten.

10-21 in 2009; 4-14 in the Big Ten.

12-20 in 2010; 3-15 in the Big Ten.

All of this added to the hype of Cody's commitment to Indiana, and throughout the season, Cody was oftentimes referred to as "Tom Crean's first big-time recruit at Indiana" and "the savior of Indiana basketball."

Indiana's rich history combined with its recent woes seemed to be the ingredients that combined to form a hurricane of hype as Cody arrived in B-Town the fall semester of his freshman year. Because of the recruits Coach Crean was landing,

CODY: I always disliked that "savior" label that people gave me. There's only one Savior—he was nailed to a cross and rose again.

there was a feeling that, for the first time in a long time, Indiana was heading in the right direction again—not just on the floor, but off the floor as well. Hoosier Nation was *desperate* to attain prominence again, and, in some ways, felt Cody held the key.

A number of things had also developed in the six years between Luke's arrival in South Bend and Cody's in Bloomington. Perhaps the most extraordinary was the explosion of social media. At any given time throughout Cody's freshman season, Lorri and I could get on Twitter, search his name, and find out the specific details of his day—whether he made it to class (because someone might tweet that they saw him on the shuttle and another might tweet that he was in their freshman business class), where he ate lunch (because someone might tweet that they saw him at Subway), and what he did that evening (because someone might tweet that they saw him shopping at Walmart). It was bizarre. Sometimes a simple thing like shopping or attending church on Sunday, judging by Twitter, seemed more like he was being tracked by the paparazzi. ❁

The other thing that always seemed to be developing was the media. There were more news avenues, more blogs, more message boards, and more interaction. There were more expectations because there were more people to create a buzz and more people to have an opinion, whether they were credible or not. Cody was oftentimes asked the question, "How do you handle all the expectations?"

CODY: It kept me out of trouble. If I did something as simple as cutting someone in the lunch line, there was a good chance that they would tweet it.

"I've had expectations my whole life," he would laugh.

And it was true.

Luke won one State title. Tyler won two. So what did Cody do? He won three.

"Plus," he'd say, "you guys [the media] are the ones making the expectations. I have no expectations."

A lot of things prepared him for IU. His brothers. Playing in the Hatchet House. The pressure he had experienced his entire life. But I also think he had the perfect personality to handle what was thrown at him. If Luke or Tyler would have been placed in his situation, who knows what might have happened?

Cody always had a knack for simplifying the chaos. If Lorri was ever concerned about something the media was saying regarding his performance, Cody might say, "Oh, it's just the media," then move on. If he had a frustrating evening on the court, he might casually laugh and say, "I was on the 'struggle bus' for a while," then move on. If it was a physical game, he might say, "The freshman couldn't get a call tonight," then move on. Cody never seemed to take himself too seriously. He would talk about himself in third person. ✹

He never allowed himself to get too high after a good performance, and he never allowed himself to sink too low after a poor performance. The pressure and expectations seemed to have no bearing on his mental and emotional well-being. He was steady. ✹

This allowed him to truly enjoy the little things in life. Sure, he loved basketball, and his teammates at Indiana are some of his best friends today. But he also noticed things that others didn't. He once sent out a tweet thanking the maintenance guys for cutting down the branch that he and all the other seven-footers were running into.

Through it all, he remained the same ol' Cody, even as the hype continued to increase at Indiana.

᠃᠃᠃

In all fairness, we feel that Cody's time at Indiana deserves our attention since it serves as a significant part of Hoosier history.

> ✹
>
> **CODY:** Cody thinks this is funny.

> ✹
>
> **CODY:** I hated it when Mom got on Twitter or read the message boards. She is a strong advocate of not reading any of them—but then she goes and reads them! Sometimes she would say, "Don't get on Twitter," after one of us had a bad game. I think it really bothered her, but none of us cared what people said about us online. I always told her, "Everyone is the same size on Twitter."
>
> I love basketball but it has never been my identity. My identity is my faith, my family,

and my education. No matter if I had a good or bad game, I always knew that my faith, my family, and my education were there for me. It took the "worry" and "pressure" out of the equation. What would my foundation be built on—an inconsistent game with a round ball or an unchanging God that promises eternal life?

Cody's situation was unique on a few levels. First, he committed to a program that was appreciably struggling. Second, he stayed more local than both Luke and Tyler. Third, he had the opportunity to go to the NBA almost immediately. All of these reasons added to the hype, and it was only amplified as his time at Indiana unfolded.

Cody's freshman year, Hoosier Nation finally started to see some fruit from all the strides Coach Crean had made the previous three years. It was a season that featured some big-time wins and put Indiana basketball back on the map.

Their biggest win of the season came in December when undefeated Indiana welcomed No. 1, undefeated Kentucky to Assembly Hall.

What made the game especially personal for our family was the fact that Tyler and UNC had lost to Kentucky one week before in Lexington, when UK's Anthony Davis had a game-winning block that left Tar Heel fans heartbroken. Lorri and I were in attendance at Rupp Arena that day, and the Kentucky fans had been obnoxious. We really hoped Cody and IU could avenge Tyler and UNC's loss to against the best team in the country.

One of the things Lorri and I noticed about Kentucky when they played UNC was that they didn't seem like the most experienced team. They were one of the most talented teams in the nation, but we felt that if IU could keep it close, there was a possibility that UK might fall apart at the end.

All day, wherever you went around Bloomington, people were fired up. At the game, the atmo-

CODY: When Mom saw at the start of the season that Kentucky was playing UNC and IU in back-to-back weeks, she called me and said she felt bad for me because Tyler was going to beat up on Anthony Davis the week before, and Davis was going to take all his anger out on me the following week. I was like, "Thanks for the encouragement, Mom."

sphere was unlike anything we had ever experienced before. We had been to several North Carolina/Duke rivalry games over the years, but the noise at the Indiana/Kentucky game was a whole notch higher. And the only reason I say that is because of how *hungry* the fans were. They *really* wanted that game. ❀

Throughout the game, Indiana did exactly what Lorri and I hoped they could do: keep it close. IU even had a double-figure lead with nine minutes to play in the second half.

With 13.9 seconds in the game, Indiana had possession with a chance to take the lead (trailing 71-70), but Victor Oladipo turned it over, and IU had to foul in order to stop the clock and put Kentucky at the free throw line. ❀

Kentucky missed the front side of the double-bonus free throw opportunity and made the second, giving them a 72-70 lead with 5.6 seconds left in the game. What happened next will forever be etched in Hoosier history.

Verdell Jones III caught the inbound pass, Cody set a ball screen around the half-court line, Verdell went the length of the floor, kicked it out to Christian Watford on the left wing, and Watford hit a buzzer-beater three-pointer to give IU the victory and send Assembly Hall and all of Hoosier Nation into pan-

❀

CODY: It was so loud in Assembly Hall that my ears would just turn off and go completely quiet. Even when we went out for warm-ups, I remember thinking, "Most universities would be happy with this atmosphere by tip-off, and it was an hour and a half before the game!"

❀

CODY: I've never told this story to the media or anything, but if you go back and watch, Jordy (Jordan Hulls) threw it to me at the elbow, and I was supposed to wait for Jordy to cut off, and then flip it to Vic (Victor Oladipo) in the corner. Coach told me that Anthony Davis was going to cheat it and I would have a lane to the basket for Vic to pass me the ball. I was so excited to score and win the game.

However, I caught the ball and drove to the basket right away. *I forgot to wait for Jordy to cut off.* The result was that it was extremely cluttered when I passed the ball to Vic—my defender was there, Jordy's defender was there, and Vic's defender was there—and that was one of the reasons why Vic turned it over. It was my fault for running the play wrong, and I was so mad at myself for doing so. We didn't even get a shot off.

demonium.

The following day, Cody read an article quoting Verdell Jones about the final play, and Cody realized that he ran *that* play wrong as well! UNC head coach Roy Williams has said it best: "Do you know the best thing about freshmen? They become sophomores." ❁

But it didn't matter. Watford made the shot, and it served as a declaration to the entire country that Indiana basketball was *back*.

Merely seconds after Watford made the shot, Lorri and I looked

over at the student section beside us (we were standing in the parents' section) and noticed that it was entirely empty. The floor was flooded. In an instant, it was as if an avalanche of people fell down the stands and onto the floor.

We enjoyed the celebration for fifteen minutes or so but, since Tyler was playing that night as well, we were hoping to get over to Cody's dorm room so we could watch the UNC game on Cody's computer. (Tyler had a really good game that night, too.) But it was nearly impossible to get out of Assembly Hall. More people were coming in than were going out. It was a gigantic party. ❁

⇑ ❁

CODY: We had two primary press breakers: "Five" and "Cowboy." In the article, I noticed that Verdell said we ran Cowboy, but the whole time, I thought we were running Five. And, not only did I think we were running Five, but I also ran Five wrong. On Five, I was supposed to set a back screen opposite of the ball (not on the ball, which is what happened). I was so out of position! I wasn't supposed to be around at all to set that screen. But it wasn't even the right play, anyway. I ran the wrong play the wrong way!

CODY: After celebrating with the students, we eventually made it back to the locker room. When Coach Crean finally came in, we were all jumping up and down. Someone got a bucket of ice water and dumped it on him. We all started cheering and huddling around Coach Crean, and that's when something horrifying happened: *Coach Crean started dancing.*

I can't even describe how horrible his dance moves were. It was, like, his version of the robot or something—but a really fast robot, like a robot with a strobe light on him. Joani (his wife) eventually stopped him and said, "Okay, okay, that's enough."

IU plowed through their non-conference schedule and entered the Big Ten season with an undefeated, 12-0 record.

Their Big Ten campaign, however, didn't start out as they hoped, as Michigan State handed the Hoosiers their first loss of the season. Cody only had 4 points and 3 rebounds, one of his worst games of his college career.

Would this Big Ten season be like the others? Or would it be different?

Cody bounced back the following game against No. 2 Ohio State, tallying 14 points in IU's 74-70 victory—a win that seemed to secure what everyone hoped to be true, that Indiana basketball had returned. After all, they had knocked off the top two teams in the country within the same month.

As IU's season continued, their improvement was evident. Their conference record improved from 3-15 the year before to 11-7 in 2011-12, and their overall record improved from 12-20 to 27-9, a jump of fifteen victories. Cody was named the Big Ten Freshman of the Year, and, though he was never wowed by accolades, we were very

CODY: I remember getting back on the bus and only having a text from Mom, Dad, and one of my close buddies. (Luke, Tyler and I usually didn't text after games; we would rather talk on the phone.) Usually, my phone would be blowing up after games with people congratulating me and telling me they thought I was great. This sounds really corny, but, being a big country fan, I remember listening to "You Find Out Who Your Friends Are" by Tim McGraw while I was on the bus. That song really hit home. Who would be around if basketball didn't exist? Would it be just Mom, Dad, and one of my friends?

proud of him.

As the year went on, something else was also happening that none of us expected: Cody's draft stock kept improving. ❊

Throughout the season, Indiana continued to demonstrate its resurgence from the depths. They advanced to the NCAA tournament and won its first tournament game since 2007, quite a drought for a program with as rich of a history as

Indiana. In the end, Kentucky defeated Indiana in the Sweet Sixteen and went on to win the national championship. Many believed that Indiana gave Kentucky their toughest battle en route to their title.

It had been an incredible year, Indiana's first in a while.

But that offseason, Cody had a decision to make.

Cody had gone through his entire freshman year believing that he had three more years left in his college career. It wasn't until the season ended that he even began to comprehend the reality that he could leave IU early and go to the NBA.

TYLER: One day, Cody and I were talking on the phone, and he started asking me about a couple of my teammates at North Carolina and whether or not I thought they would stay at UNC or enter the NBA Draft. "Well, what about you?" I said. "Have you thought about going to the NBA?" He told me that he honestly hadn't thought about it, and I could tell that he hadn't. He told me that he didn't even know he had a chance.

That was one of the primary reasons he decided to come back to Indiana for his sophomore season—he wanted to enjoy college more.

On top of that, Jordan Hulls, Christian Watford, and Derek Elston were entering their senior seasons, and he wanted to be there for their final year. After losing to Kentucky in the tournament the year before, they felt like they were extremely close to doing something special as a team. Cody also wanted to get another academic year under his belt so he would be closer to earning his degree.

Cody's decision to return for his sophomore campaign combined with Indiana's No. 1 preseason ranking, its first in thirty-three years, led to a whole new level of hype we had never experienced before. Cody was on the cover of *Sports Illustrated, ESPN The Magazine,* and *Sporting News.* ✪

Indiana was getting so much media attention that you would have thought they had won a national championship. ✪

Returning to the opening metaphor about the egg, potato, and coffee, I'm not sure if Cody could be compared to any of the objects dropped into the water. In the boiling water, in the heat of the hype, he just remained exactly the same. His humor, humility and the way he enjoyed life through the simplest of things didn't change, whether it was the local hype when he decided to go to Indiana or the national hype when Indiana was named the No. 1 team in the country. The expectations were always high, but he just had a go-with-the-flow attitude and took each thing as it came, enjoying each thing as it came. He remained unashamedly himself, enjoying the little things and never thinking too big of himself.

CODY: I was just disappointed that I wasn't on the cover of the *Sports Illustrated's* swimsuit edition. I was confused.

CODY: We knew we were No. 1 at the beginning of the season, but we wanted to be No. 1 at the end of the season. We knew how good we could be, and that fueled us. Our team chemistry and work ethic was really special. We would sometimes have fistfights in practice, but then we would all go get something to eat together afterwards.

One thing I've always appreciated about Cody's mindset is his ability to stay in the present. Though in the back of his mind he figured his sophomore year would probably be his final season, he continued to live his life as a student-athlete at Indiana. ✹

Sometimes, for example, his teammates would ask him to hang out after a game, and he might tell them he couldn't because he had a test the next day. They would playfully make fun of him and say,

CODY: I still bought plenty of Little Caesars $5 pizzas.

"Cody, you're going to be a lottery pick. You don't need to ace every single test!" But Cody knew nothing was guaranteed. All it took was one injury to put his entire NBA career in jeopardy. ✹

I believe that staying in the present, living in the now, is crucial in making the most of any phase of your life. And that's exactly what happened for Cody his sophomore year at Indiana.

The biggest accomplishment of the Hoosiers' 2012-13 campaign was their Big Ten regular season title, IU's first outright Big Ten title in two decades. They made it tough on themselves, however. With an

CODY: My academic advisor would ask me, "Do you want to drop by and make your academic schedule for next fall?" And I would be like, "Yeah, sure." My teammates would tell me, "There's no way you are going to be here!"

opportunity to clinch the title against Ohio State in the second-to-last game of the season, the Hoosiers lost a heartbreaker on senior night at Assembly Hall. This meant Indiana would have to beat No. 7 Michigan in Ann Arbor the final game of the regular season to seize the outright title; Michigan would share the title with a victory of its own.

The Hoosiers seemed to have their backs against the wall. Losing to Ohio State at home was a missed opportunity, and they were going up against a Michigan team that was playing its best ball of the season.

The Wolverines were also hungry. In early February, they were the top-ranked team in the country, but then Indiana dethroned them with an 81-73 victory on ESPN College Gameday at Assembly Hall to earn back the No. 1 ranking. Michigan was undoubtedly one of the best teams in the nation. How difficult would it be to beat them twice in a single season?

The entire game was a back-and-forth contest. Both teams were relentless. Looking back, it's crazy to think about how much talent was on the floor that game. Michigan had Trey Burke (ninth pick, 2013), Tim Hardaway Jr. (twenty-fourth pick, 2013), Nik Stauskas (eighth pick, 2014), Mitch McGary (twenty-first pick, 2014), and Glenn Robinson III (fortieth pick, 2014). Indiana had Victor Oladipo (second pick, 2013), Cody (fourth pick, 2013), Christian Watford (Israel, 2013), Jordan Hulls (Poland, 2013), Derek Elston (Italy, 2013), and Will Sheehey (Montenegro, 2014).

Lorri and I weren't together for the game—she was in Phoenix for a week with Luke and Hope, as Hope was due with their first child and our first grandchild. We texted each other throughout the game, however, like we always did

CODY: Before the game, Vic and I told Coach Crean that neither of us wanted to come out of the game. We said, "Coach, we'll tell you when we want to come out of the game. We condition so hard during the season to prepare for games like this! Leave us in."

The Kentucky game my freshman year was very memorable, but when people today ask me about my most memorable game, I tell them that it was at Michigan for the Big Ten championship.

CODY: One of the questions that NBA scouts and general managers would always ask is, "How do you want to be remembered?" or some variation of that question. My answer was always, "I want to be remembered as a winner."

In high school, it was neat to win Mr. Basketball, but I was most proud of my three State championships because I know that it took an entire team to win those championships. At IU, it was neat to be on the cover of

Sports Illustrated and to be recognized as one of the top players in the country, but all I cared about was winning. Needless to say, I wanted to win that game at Michigan for the Big Ten championship REALLY BAD!

Trailing 71-70, Cody scored a layup to give IU a 72-71 lead with 13.7 seconds remaining in the game. Michigan's Player of the Year, Trey Burke, missed a layup on the other end, and Jordan Morgan tried to tip it in for the Wolverines—the ball seemed to hang on the rim for a year. But it never dropped, and IU won its first outright title since 1993. ✹

when we weren't together.

The game was tied with under two minutes to play, but two Michigan buckets gave them a five-point advantage with only fifty seconds to go.

Somehow, Indiana willed its way back into the game. ✹

CODY: Later, someone told me that they had already rolled Michigan's Big Ten championship trophy out of the tunnel at the corner of the arena.

It was the craziest fifty seconds of basketball of my life!

CODY: I pride myself on not worrying about things that I can't control, especially things in the past. But in that moment, I remember thinking of everything that I had done in the past to reach that point—all the hours that I had spent in the gym, all the people who had helped me on and off the court, every coach that had taught me since I started playing, all the games that I had played in, all the practices throughout the years, all the conditioning tests that I suffered through, all the days of lifting weights, and every six o'clock in the morning workout dating back to junior high. It had all helped me reach a point where I could sit in the locker in Michigan and say out loud to myself, "I'm a Big Ten champion."

Lorri told Hope, "If that baby doesn't come after all this excitement, that baby is never going to come."

Of course, the baby did arrive . . . several weeks later.

〰〰

After starting the season ranked No. 1 in the country, IU lived up to the hype throughout the season and was awarded a No. 1 seed in the NCAA tournament. Unfortunately, IU underperformed in the tournament, falling in the Sweet Sixteen to Syracuse, who went on to advance to the Final Four.

Following the season, Cody decided to make a decision that neither of his brothers made and enter the NBA Draft early as a sophomore. We felt Cody had a good handle on the situation, and, just like his decision to attend Indiana, it was his decision whether or not he wanted to enter the NBA Draft.

One primary reason for entering the draft was that we had seen Tyler sit through the draft the year before and had learned that he fell on the draft board because he was older than many of the earlier picks.

Tyler's draft was a great experience, but I know it was nerve-racking at times for him. I remember ten picks going by without any selection, and with each subsequent pick, Tyler started chomping on ice more and more in the green room. A waiter kept bringing him water, and Tyler would drink the water quickly, then nervously chomp on a mouthful of ice. After the sixteenth pick, ice was literally flying out of his mouth. I was playing with a paper football and seeing how far I could flick it, which was fun.

The Dallas Mavericks eventually selected him seventeenth overall before trading him to the Cleveland Cavaliers. We were so proud of him.

When Cody was deciding whether to enter the draft, an NBA general manager told me that much of the draft is based on how they project your potential. They want to know where each player will be in seven years—they consider this the player's prime. This is why they are sometimes more drawn to younger players. By your third year in the NBA you should start producing, and by your seventh year you should be at the top of your game. Using this formula, Cody would start producing a year after Tyler, but he would be much younger. NBA GMs want to see how many "extra" years they can get out of you, another reason why youth is such a key component.

The GM had some funny stories, too. He said that one time he was explaining to a player how half of his $1 million contract would go to taxes and the player replied, "I didn't sign up for taxes."

Overall, what Cody learned was that there really wasn't much of an option for him to stay at Indiana, logically. Since he was predicted to be a lottery pick in the upcoming draft, he would have had to improve exponentially during his junior year, just to move up the draft board minimally. He would improve much more as a player competing against guys in the NBA. Also, from a financial standpoint, he found it difficult to turn down a million-dollar job offer. In an interview leading up to the draft, ESPN's Bill Simmons asked Cody what his first purchase would be, and Cody replied that he would "probably just save it all." Just like his time at IU, we were proud of the way he carried himself as he transitioned into his professional career.

The evening of the draft, Cody had a good feeling about the Charlotte Bobcats (now the Hornets), who had the fourth overall selection. He was especially excited when his Indiana teammate, Victor Oladipo, was selected No. 2 overall by the Orlando Magic. We were with Cody in the green room at the Barclays Center in Brooklyn, New York.

The fourth pick eventually rolled around, and Charlotte had five minutes to make a selection.

"This could be me," Cody said to Lorri and me. Cody started looking over at his agent, Sam Goldfeder, who was sitting nearby. ❉

Four minutes.

Three minutes. ❉

Two minutes.

One minute.

TYLER: Whenever I was selected the year before, Sam was able to tell me the situation before the announcement was made. Cody had a lot of questions leading up to the draft, and I told him that Sam would be able to guide him and inform him, just as he did with me.

CODY: Sam was just sitting there, no worries in the world. He was looking out at the crowd—not how you would picture an agent to act.

"Well," Cody said to Lorri and me, "looks like they are going to pass on me." ✱

NBA commissioner David Stern stepped up to the podium and announced, "With the fourth pick in the 2013 NBA Draft, the Charlotte Bobcats select Cody Zeller from Indiana University." ✱

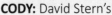

CODY: Sam didn't even have his phone in his hand. It was just resting on the table. He wasn't even looking at me.

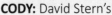

CODY: David Stern's announcement was the first time I heard the news. Sam eventually said to me, "I knew a while ago. I just wanted to make you worry and play a joke on *you* for once."

"I probably deserved that," I said.

wwww

Enjoying the Ride

Cody's decision to leave Indiana early was another reminder for us to make the most of each moment and enjoy each phase of our journey as parents.

I'm a firm believer that just about everything in life must be approached on the grounds of enjoyment. It's as if everything we experience—the big things and the little things, the mountaintops and the valleys—are opportunities to enjoy, experience, and rest in God in a new and different way. ✱

And that's one reason why we felt the urgency to attend as many games as we possibly could as Luke was grinding his way through Notre Dame, Tyler ventured through North Carolina, and Cody spent two years at Indiana. We didn't want to miss out. One day, this

CODY: The way Mom and Dad approach life reminds me of Travis Tritt's country song, "It's a Great Day to be Alive."

phase would also pass. They were experiences we didn't want to take for granted—especially ever since the wake-up call we received Tyler's freshman year when we thought he might have a career-ending wrist injury. Like every phase of life, it was a gift that was to be enjoyed.

Cody would oftentimes tell us throughout high school, "I don't know why you travel around so much when you could sit on the sofa and watch the exact same thing at home."

Lorri would always tell him, "Since Tyler's injury, I don't want to miss out on anything ever again."

WWW

When it comes to enjoying the ride, the story that stands out to me the most is from Tyler's senior year at North Carolina and Cody's freshman season at Indiana.

Both the Tar Heels and Hoosiers were playing in the Big Ten/ACC Challenge down in Carolina, and, from the start, Lorri was afraid Tyler and Cody were going to have to play against one another. Luke and Tyler were suppose to play against each other Luke's senior season at Notre Dame in the Maui Invitational, but Tyler hurt his wrist, so it never happened. With it being Tyler's senior season, people figured that the Big Ten/ACC Challenge might be the final opportunity for a pair of the Zeller brothers to face each other in the collegiate realm if the two teams didn't meet in the NCAA tournament—which was unlikely.

The only thing I didn't like about the idea of our boys' facing one another was the attention swirling around it within the two fan bases. When Luke and Tyler were supposed to face each other in the Maui Invitational, both Notre Dame and North Carolina fans made it a somewhat big deal about which side we would sit on. This was an uncomfortable place to be in. But, other than that, I secretly kind of wanted our boys to face each other.

Lorri, on the other hand, dreaded the idea. She felt those match-ups were for our eyes only. Luckily for Lorri, Indiana and North Carolina didn't end up facing each other in the Big Ten/ACC Challenge. ✻

However, they did end up playing on the same evening in gymnasiums that were twenty-five miles apart.

CODY: Tyler is lucky, too.

We started thinking . . . could we attend both games?

Indiana was playing NC State at a quarter after seven in Raleigh, and North Carolina was playing Wisconsin at nine thirty in Chapel Hill. We decided to go for it. We would attend the first two-thirds of Cody's game and then make the half-hour drive to catch Tyler's game. ESPN heard about what we were trying to do, found it unique, and decided to cover our evening and update their viewers on our progress and whereabouts. Lorri and I decided to wear T-shirts that the home economics teacher at Washington High School, Mrs. Thompson, had made for us—a split T-shirt with Tar Heel blue on the right side and Hoosier crimson on the left side.

Indiana was 6-0 entering the game, and their matchup on the road against the 5-1 NC State Wolfpack was, by far, their most difficult challenge in their early season. Indiana trailed the Wolfpack 42-41 at halftime and fell behind by seven points with less than eight minutes left in the game, NC State's biggest lead in the contest. We left the RBC Center soon after to make it in time for Tyler's game and weren't sure if Indiana was going to be able to come back. We were forced to leave with a bitter taste in our mouths.

ESPN cameras showed us leaving the game, and they created a subplot to its viewers as to whether we would make it to Tyler's game on time. With ESPN timing us, we (Lorri and two of our friends) decided to take the back roads to Chapel Hill to make quicker time.

Of course, on the way there, we got stuck behind a gigantic dump truck on a winding two-lane country road, making it impossible for us to pass it.

"Hurry up!" Lorri said. "ESPN is timing us!"

As the dump truck tried to prevent us from arriving in Chapel Hill (the driver was probably a Duke fan), we listened to the remainder of Cody's game on the radio. Cody scored eight immediate points and helped spark a 20-7 Hoosier run to close the game and defeat NC State—a huge Hoosier win.

After the game, the media asked Cody about the timing of the comeback. It literally took place right when Lorri and I left the arena. He told them, "Maybe they shouldn't have come at all. We might have won by twenty."

Leave it to Cody to find humor in everything that happens.

By the time we arrived at the Dean Dome, we couldn't find a place to park. The NCAA prohibits universities from giving any of the players' parents any perks or special privileges, and that included preferred parking. Entering our adventure, we knew that finding parking might be a challenge—especially since we'd be arriving last minute. We eventually ended up finding a spot in a parking garage a half-mile away, but it meant we would have to run to the gymnasium if we wanted to make it in time for the tip-off. Also, Lorri was wearing high-heel boots. Miracle she didn't twist an ankle.

As we arrived at the Dean Dome after running the 800-meter dash for the first time since high school gym class, ESPN's cameras caught us entering the gymnasium.

"The Zellers have arrived in time," the broadcaster said.

I'm sure if their cameras had zoomed in more, they would have seen our clothing and faces drenched in sweat. I'm sure our faces betrayed exhaustion. We were wiped. But it was an adventure nonetheless, and we had a blast doing it. We also walked away from the evening with two victories, as No. 5 North Carolina defeated No. 9 Wisconsin 60-57 to improve to 6-1 on the season.

When the media interviewed Tyler after the game, they asked him about our little escapade, and he basically told them that he thought we were crazy.

"They're nuts," he told them.

Since Tyler's scary injury his freshman year, we had come a long way.

One of the best questions you can ask in this life and in the context of parenting is: Why not?

There are all sorts of excuses and reasons *not* to do something. And the reasons will *always* be there.

"There isn't enough time."

"There's too much to do."

"It costs too much money."

"People will think we are crazy."

Like most meaningful things in this life, every adventure we have embarked on has seemed to always

TYLER: No, you guys *are* crazy.

195

require two things: sacrifice and discomfort. But that's what makes it an adventure.

We afforded going to their games by sacrificing other things. We never felt like we needed to have name-brand clothing, a fancy house, or drive the newest car. We hardly ever flew to games. We drove everywhere (except Hawaii, of course) because it was so much cheaper than two airplane tickets. We very carefully allocated our days off from work and tried to do most of our traveling on weekends. We used our vacation time and took half days to see our children.

Maybe seeing two games in one night is only a silly story, but it also seems to represent the way Lorri and I try to approach our daily lives. It was just another experience, another story in the greater adventure. Even if she was running a half-mile to the Dean Dome in high-heel boots as ESPN timed us.

LUKE: I can't tell you how many times Dad would drive up to South Bend for a game in the middle of the week, get back to Washington in the middle of the night, and then be back at work early the next morning. It meant a lot to me.

It gave us something to write about, didn't it?

CODY: Wish I could have seen that!

Experiences and adventures are never easy. They are not meant to be. There are no guarantees—the unknown, actually, makes each adventure fun. That's what makes it a new experience. To keep using the same anecdote, it wasn't easy driving to North Carolina—it would have been easier to stay at home and flip back and forth between both games on the couch. It wasn't easy to leave Cody's game with eight minutes left—it would have been easier to stay there. It wasn't easy running to the Dean Dome—it would have been easier to take our time, walk to the gymnasium, and arrive a few minutes late. But we were determined. We were invested. And the more you invest in something, the more opportunity you have to experience a greater adventure. If we had done what was easy, what was convenient, which cost less money, which used less energy, we wouldn't have had the memories. There's nothing compelling in a story about the time you watched both Indiana and North Carolina win while eating a bag of chips and sipping a soda on your couch.

The bottom line is that *you* make the choices of what you can and can't do. Time doesn't always decide what you can and can't do. Your to-do list doesn't always decide what you can and can't do. Your bank account doesn't always decide what you can and can't do. We were both working full-time jobs, but we sacrificed sleep. We both had plenty to do back in Washington, but we changed the priorities on our to-do list. We spent a lot of money traveling the country—watching Luke, Tyler, and Cody both at home and on the road—but we cut our budget in other areas.

As Lorri always says, this life isn't a dress rehearsal. Parenting isn't a dress rehearsal. It's a great adventure, a one-time-only adventure. It's a ride that is to be enjoyed. And sometimes, it takes sacrifice. The thing is, when it's people you love, it hardly feels like sacrifice. Nothing is more valuable, both for yourself and for your children, than presence.

Something to remember about presence is that it sometimes has much more to do with the emotional than the physical. For example, a parent might return home from work at a decent time, but as he or she sits around the dinner table that evening, his or her mind might be elsewhere. The parent might be present physically but isn't present emotionally. It's a challenge to be fully present because there is so much going on in each of our worlds—our to-do lists sometimes feel never-ending—but your children and family deserve your very all and, not only that, you deserve to experience all of your family. It's impossible to experience all of your family if you are not fully engaged.

Consider our spiritual lives. God wants our very all, but the great mystery is that we will experience more of God the more we give to Him. It's one thing to attend church on Sunday morning and sit in the congregation (you are indeed physically present with your body), but you will probably learn a lot more about God if you focus on what is being communicated through words from the pulpit or lyrics in a song—your emotional and mental presence, your soul.

When it comes to daily living, giving God our very all, our very being, consequently brings more hope, joy, and peace to our own lives because God is the fountain of all of these things. Serving the needy, reading your Bible, and going to church aren't practices you check off your to-do list; rather, they are ways—chances, opportunities, invitations—to experience God more. Similarly, giving your very all to your family—your spouse and your children, or your mother and your father—allows you to experience them more.

Full presence is the key to building relationships in this life, whether it be with your family or friends, because it frees up your heart and mind to invest in the lives of others. If you sit around the dinner table at night and your mind is still thinking about your work at the office, you're technically still absorbed in your own little world and not the more meaningful world that you share with others. Nothing is more meaningful than walking alongside others and enjoying life *with* them.

Every day is an opportunity to invest in something meaningful, embark on an adventure, and enhance your story. We all have twenty-four hours in any given day. I have always felt that saying, "I don't have time" is a poor excuse. If something is truly important to me, I always seem able to make time for it. It's all about how we choose to use the time available to us. I once read that during our lifetime, we are creating a "bank of memories." Some day, when we are no longer physically able to do such things, we will have a bank of memories to draw back upon and enjoy.

As our children went on to play college basketball at Division I universities—Luke at Notre Dame, Tyler at North Carolina, and Cody at Indiana—we decided that sitting on the couch and watching each of their games, though it might be easier, cheaper, and more convenient, would not be treating this life as a great adventure. Rather, it would be treating it as if it were a dress rehearsal. We wanted to enjoy the ride to the fullest. To us, that meant attending our children's college basketball games any time we could, something that we considered a unique privilege and blessing.

It's far too easy to take this life for granted—to wake up each morning hoping to survive the day rather than striving to seize it, to go through life acting as a victim rather than living as a blessed child of God, to journey through life succumbing to its demands rather than enjoying its challenges.

Eventually, we will all be dropped in the boiling water—it is inevitable. Challenges in this life are actually quite normal and expected. And so much of your life will be influenced by how you react to adversity.

This life isn't a dress rehearsal. It's the real thing. It might as well be enjoyed, treasured, and approached with a sense of severity—that the decisions we make and opportunities in our paths have meaning and significance.

In each and every phase, enjoy the ride.

1.0 THE HEART OF IT ALL
by Lorri Zeller

As Steve said, there is nothing more valuable than presence, both for yourself and for your children, and presence comes in several different forms. Physical. Emotional. Spiritual.

Why, then, if life is all about relationships, do we think we can venture through this journey of life on our own, without the help of others, without the presence of others?

At the same time Luke was going through Notre Dame, Steve and I also experienced the boiling water, and I thought I could handle it alone.

In early 2007, Steve and I decided to focus on getting in shape. We started exercising daily, and we each lost about forty pounds in a single summer. I started to feel much healthier, but Steve, oddly, started to feel worse. In fact, the more he pushed himself during a workout, the worse his physical condition seemed to be. He became convinced that it was impossible for him to get in shape. He struggled to breathe. And he struggled to make any progression in his workouts.

One day, while playing basketball against the boys in the Hatchet House, Steve blacked out. ✹

LUKE: It was the end of the summer before my fall semester at Notre Dame, and Dad and I were playing against Tyler and Cody one Sunday afternoon. I usually guarded Tyler, and Dad always did a good job of bodying up Cody and sticking with him. This particular day, however, Cody kept back-cutting and getting layups. It was the worst I had ever seen Dad play. I didn't understand why he kept making the same mistake over and over again. Several weeks later, he admitted that he kept blacking out while we were playing. Dad, being a tough guy, didn't want to say anything.

He knew something was wrong, and he went to the doctor to see if doctors could discover what the problem was.

٭٭٭

Steve hardly ever called me during the day on my office line at Washington High School. And when he called me one fall day in 2008, I wondered what the issue could be.

"They know what's wrong with my heart," he told me when he called.

"Okay . . . " I said cautiously.

"Are you sitting down?" he asked.

"Yeah," I said, wondering how bad it could possibly be. "There's nothing you can say that's going to make me upset," I told him.

"Well," he said, "I have a bad valve. And I have to get surgery to replace it."

I didn't say much. I was scared.

"Sounds serious," I eventually said.

٭٭٭

It was serious enough that doctors scheduled the surgery as soon as they could—open-heart, within two weeks. He was told to "lay low" and not do anything physical until the surgery. ٭

Luke was entering his junior year at Notre Dame at the time, Tyler was a senior in high school, and Cody was a freshman. Over the years, we had seen some difficult circumstanc-

CODY: That might have been true, but I remember Dad climbing a tree to rescue a cat just a couple of days before his surgery. He went on with his normal life. He didn't want to seem weak.

LUKE: I also remember doing a high-ropes course with Dad and Cody—forty feet up in the air—merely days before his doctor's visit. Looking back, I doubt he should have been doing that.

_____

es in Washington, but we hadn't really dealt with anything in regard to our immediate family. This was new for us.

Each of the boys had his own reaction leading up to the surgery. Luke took the spiritual route and said he would be praying for Steve. Tyler, of course, didn't say anything about the surgery and kept to himself. I finally asked him, "Aren't you worried?"

"There's no need to worry," he told me.

"Why is that?" I said.

"The surgery will either be successful, and he will be fine," Tyler said, "or he will die and go to heaven. So . . . why worry?"

"I don't really like Option B," I told Tyler.

"Well, he's going to be fine either way," he said.

Do you worry about anything? I remember thinking.

Cody, of course, made a joke out of it.

"You better hope that I don't visit you," he told Steve, "because if I do, I'm just going to pull the plug and put you out of your misery."

I am convinced I will never understand men.

ⱳⱲⱮ

Over the next two weeks, I tried not to think about it. I distracted myself with work and the kids and treated life as if I wasn't counting down the days.

The Friday before his heart surgery, Steve drove to the high school on his break to have lunch with me. When he walked into the athletic office, he had a look on his face that I hadn't seen before.

"Everything all right?" I asked.

"Yeah," he said, scratching his head, "I just had the strangest thing happen to me."

"What do you mean?" I asked.

"Well, ya know Dave Manzer?"

"Yeah, of course," I said.

Dave Manzer was a basketball trainer that all of our boys worked with at different times in Indianapolis. We hadn't heard from him in a while.

"Well," Steve continued, "he called me out of the blue and told me he had heard about my surgery. Then, at the end of our conversation, he said to me, 'Steve, can I pray with you over the phone?'"

Praying over the phone was not something we had ever done. I could tell that Steve was deeply impacted by the conversation, and he went on to tell me about the nature of the prayer. He said it went something like this:

> *Heavenly Father, we come to You to thank You for all that You have given us. You have taught Steve that he doesn't have to worry, because You are in control. You have a plan and you knew what Steve's life was going to be from beginning to end, before Steve was ever born. You know the outcome of this surgery, and You know that Steve's family will be taken care of because Steve has taught them to love You. Give Steve the courage to trust You and all of the angels that you will send. Steve knows that the hands that will touch him both physically and spiritually are Your hands. It will be such a joy to live through this knowing that You are so close. Thank You Lord for the peace that You have given Steve, and I know that Steve will give all the glory back to You. I say this prayer in Jesus' name. Amen.*

One year later, Dave passed away due to complications during a heart surgery that was very similar to Steve's.

Luke insisted that he join me at the hospital in the waiting room instead of driving up to start his fall semester at Notre Dame, but I shrugged off his urgency and told him that the surgery would go just fine. I would call him afterward. Plus, he had class and basketball conditioning, and I told him I didn't want him to miss either of them.

I finally told Luke that, if he wanted to help, he could stay in Washington and watch over Tyler and Cody. They wanted to join me in the waiting room, too, but I didn't want them to miss school. Plus, Cody had a tennis match that evening.

Everyone seemed to be making Steve's surgery a bigger deal than I thought it was—or maybe I was just avoiding how big a deal it really was? ✿

I just figured I'd sit in the waiting room, read a magazine, and listen to some music—it'd be fine. In no time, his surgery would be complete. I was a big girl—and, if I was going to worry about something, then I just wanted to worry about it by myself.

LUKE: It definitely seemed like Mom was trying to downplay everything.

The day of his surgery finally came.

We woke up early the morning of August 27, 2007, and left Washington at 3:53 a.m.—I remember seeing that exact time on the radio display in our van as we pulled out of our driveway. There was also a beautiful full moon in the sky, and it seemed to guide us south toward Evansville like a lantern.

Our drive was just like any other drive. We had country music faintly playing in the background on the radio and talked to one another as we always did—about the boys, about his job at Perdue Foods, about my job in the athletic department, and about people.

It was just another day. We didn't talk about his surgery or anything related to it, but I, of course was worried for him. If I could have taken his place, I certainly would have. I would rather go through the procedure than be the one watching from the outside. But we were also ready to face the challenge and face it together.

We arrived at St. Mary's Hospital in Evansville at five o'clock and checked in so they could perform his blood work and give him medicine. Our pastor from church soon arrived at the hospital (I couldn't talk him out of coming), and he prayed with Steve and me in the waiting room before all the procedures began. At seven thirty, the anesthesiologist came in and visited, and a few minutes later, the surgical crew took Steve away. My pastor and I, then, moved to the

Cardiovascular Intensive Care waiting room. Our pastor insisted on staying with me—I couldn't make him leave.

Once Steve entered surgery at eight in the morning, I called the boys and told them things were underway. None of the boys asked many questions. Luke said he would be praying and asked once again if I wanted company in the waiting room. I told him it wasn't a big deal and that I would give him another call later. Soon, it'd be over. Our call ended, and I took a deep breath, exhaled, and looked around the waiting room. ✵

St. Mary's only had one gigantic waiting room for all the procedures taking place. I could tell that some of the families and friends of the patients had been there for a long time—for some, it looked like days—while others would be in and out in a couple of hours for some of the more minor procedures. I knew this place would be my home for the next couple of days due to the severity of Steve's surgery. It was a purgatory of sorts. There was no privacy. Just souls that wanted out. And now, I was one of them.

Lofted in the corner of the waiting room was a large, flat-screen monitor that showed the progress of

CODY: I tried to convince myself throughout the day that everything was going to be all right—attempting to go about my normal schedule and keep my mind off Dad's procedure. However, I sometimes couldn't help but think about the chance that Dad might not make it through. Obviously, you try to keep your thoughts positive, and I knew that he was strong, but I couldn't imagine a life without my dad.

each patient, detailing whether they were in (1) Pre-Op Surgery, (2) Anesthesia, (3) Surgery, or (4) Recovery. Over the next hour, my eyes went back and forth between the flat-screen television and the time displayed on my cell phone. Never before had I seen time move so slowly. I wondered if time was even moving.

At 9:02, I received a call from the operating room, telling me that Steve had been placed on the bypass machine. This is the most dangerous phase of the surgery because the heart is removed and the bypass machine takes over the function of the heart. Before the surgery, I had read in a pamphlet that a patient's risk of a stroke dramatically increases if he's on the machine for more than an hour.

This was all extremely weird to me—incomprehensible, really. I didn't know how to deal with the fact that, somehow, Steve wasn't actually alive (was he?) because his heart had been removed—something that had been beating his entire life. I just knew I felt scared or uncomfortable or anxious or something.

All I could do was pray and watch the clock on my phone, a clock that hardly seemed to change. Time was quickly becoming my worst enemy. The more time that elapsed, the more doubts formed in my mind. I felt both bound to it and helpless in its grasp. And it was only the first hour of his surgery!

Fortunately, several visitors started to drop by the waiting room—friends from church and school whom I apparently couldn't talk out of coming. Their presence helped distract me from the clock, though my eyes were still continually drawn to it like a magnet. I frequently looked up at the flat-screen television, only to see "Surgery" next to Steve's name over and over again.

Within the first hour that Steve was on bypass, a particular visitor approached me wearing a badge and dressed in a suit. The badge made me think he might be clergy, and my mind immediately drew the worst conclusion imaginable—that something had happened to Steve in the most dangerous part of the surgery. He cautiously and slowly approached me, and I couldn't take my eyes off him. He gave me the feeling that the Grim Reaper was approaching me, dressed in a suit. What did he want? What news was he bearing? I didn't know him, so why was he there?

"Mrs. Zeller?" he questioned.

I hesitated to even say, "Yes?"

He proceeded to introduce himself as a friend of one of the coaches at Notre Dame, and he happened to work in food service at the hospital. His badge was merely a hospital badge. All he was doing was bringing me a handful of coupons for free meals at the hospital over the coming days. It was a kind gesture, though I doubt that I adequately expressed how thankful I was because of how overcome with fear I had been.

My mind was playing tricks on me.

〰️🌾

At 9:50 a.m., I received a call from the operating room, and the nurse told me all was going well.

But then another hour passed.

As I had read, the chance for a stroke dramatically increases after only an hour on the bypass machine—but Steve had been on it, now, for nearly two hours!

I wondered why it was taking them so long. What was going on?

Finally, around eleven thirty, I received another call from the operating room, and the nurse told me Steve had been taken off the machine—finally. I saw his status on the television screen change from "Surgery" to "Recovery," and I breathed a huge sigh of relief.

Thirty minutes later, Steve's doctor, Dr. Bucshon, came into the waiting room and told me about the surgery. He said it went well—they had put in a new valve—but Steve's valve was in worse shape than the pre-surgery heart catheterization test indicated. He said the flaps on the valve should be like "tissue paper" but Steve's were as "hard as rock." They also put in a new aorta because the old aorta was ballooned and pear-shaped. His new aorta, Dr. Bucshon explained, was made out of Dacron tubing, a synthetic polyester textile fiber.

Dr. Bucshon was so well spoken and confident in the way he explained everything to me, despite the unexpected issues he encountered during the procedure, that I naturally felt relieved and comforted after our conversation. He viewed the surgery as so routine that he called it a "meat and potatoes procedure." He was so casual about it all you would have thought he found the "Dacron tubing" for Steve's aorta in an aisle at Lowe's.

The only complication they were facing, Dr. Bucshon explained, was some bleeding that they were keeping an eye on, but it didn't seem to be a big concern of his. He said I would be able to see Steve soon.

I called Luke, texted Cody and Tyler since they were in school, and reached out to several of my closest friends to tell them Steve's surgery had gone well. My pastor led us in a prayer of thanksgiving, praising God for carrying Steve through the surgery and me through the procedures. ❂

Now, all I had to do was wait for the doctor to give me permission to see Steve. And I couldn't wait.

〜〜

Maybe I'm just not a patient person. I don't know.

But my mind began playing more tricks on me the longer I waited for the doctor to call me. Steve's surgery had ended at twelve thirty, and I had finished talking to our pastor and all of the friends and family by two thirty. It had been two hours, and I still wasn't able to see Steve. They kept telling me that Steve was "getting settled in." I knew Steve would be practically unconscious and definitely unresponsive, but I wanted to *see* him and know he was okay, know that his heart was beating. Why the delay? Was this normal? Or was my mind continuing to play tricks on me?

Dr. Bucshon finally called me around three o'clock and told me I could see him. I asked him if something was wrong. He told me Steve was losing a lot of blood, approximately a cup per hour. As a result, they were giving him platelets and keeping him on the ventilator.

He also warned me that Steve was probably going to look a lot different right after surgery. He was right. Steve was swollen from all the fluids being pumped into him, and Dr. Bucshon explained to me that he had a tube running down his throat and another one running down his back behind his heart for drainage.

It was very eerie standing over Steve's bed. Steve was much like his father and my father—a man's man who hardly ever showed vulnerability or weakness. Standing over his bed, as he lay there unconscious, unable to breathe on his own, bleeding internally, my feeling was that this was by far the weakest I had ever seen him.

I also noticed a container next to his bed that was steadily collecting blood. I couldn't take my eyes off it. As gross as it was, I couldn't stop looking at it. I wondered when it would stop. When would they get the bleeding under control?

LUKE: Mom called me and told me the surgery was a success. Her tone really made it seem as if it wasn't a big deal. In the back of my mind, I was thinking, "Surgery on the aorta sounds like a pretty big deal."

One of two things needed to happen: They needed to get him off the ventilator, or they needed the bleeding to slow down. Neither, however, was happening. Every time they tried to take him off the ventilator, the bleeding would increase.

An hour passed.

And another.

And another.

Nothing changed. His situation had not improved at all; in fact, it was only worsening. His amount of bleeding was so abnormal, I became extremely worried that he was bleeding to death.

The surgeon remained by Steve's bedside the entire time, monitoring his blood loss and preparing for the possibility that they were going to take him back into surgery.

Before this development, I had called my closest friends and the boys and told them that the surgery had gone well. I had even prayed with our pastor and thanked God for carrying Steve through the surgery. Merely hours before, I had felt immense relief. And now I felt more anxious than ever.

I was scared. And I felt alone. ❖

Desperate for some sort of counsel, I decided to consult a Bloomington cardiologist and seek his medical advice. His name was Dr. Larry Rink, and he was a family friend of ours. He also worked closely with Indiana University athletics. I was trying to further understand the seriousness of the situation and decipher whether or not I was overreacting. I called Dr. Rink on his cell phone, and he took my call even though he was on vacation with his family in Hawaii. I could tell by Dr. Rink's reaction that the situation was as serious as I believed it to be, if not more so, and he suggested that I give the boys a call and bring the family in.

I was tired of being "superwoman" and trying to go through the

CODY: It's crazy to think that Mom was feeling all of this, and none of us boys had any idea.

TYLER: We were just going through our daily routines.

situation by myself. Even though some of my friends were there, it wasn't the same as having my three children next to me. I began questioning myself. Why hadn't I allowed them to come? Why did I think I could go through something like this on my own?

All I wanted was Luke, Tyler, and Cody to be sitting next to me.

I wanted my family.

꽃

I gave Luke a call.

When he answered, he was on his way back to South Bend. ✤

I gave Tyler a call, and told him that a couple of our friends from Washington were going to bring him the hospital.

Cody had just finished his tennis match, so Luke met up with the team bus on the side of the road to pick up Cody and go to the hospital. ✤

꽃

At seven o'clock in the evening or so, I visited Steve again. He still couldn't talk, but he was more responsive than before. He listened to

LUKE: Since Mom had told me that afternoon that the surgery had gone well, I decided to head back to Notre Dame so I could make it to class the next day. When she called a second time, I immediately turned around. The call was short, but she sounded extremely panicked—the exact opposite of the first call. Hearing Mom's tone made me panic, too. I immediately pulled over and started texting everyone on my contact list: "Please pray. My dad needs prayers." I also called Coach Brey and he told me, "Take all the time you need. The most important thing right now is for you to focus on your family." That meant a lot to me.

CODY: When I got off the bus and saw Luke, all he said to me was, "We have to go see Dad."

everything I said and winked at me. He held my thumb and shook his head "yes" when I told him that a lot of people were praying for him. Again, I noticed the plastic container next to his bed filling up with blood at the same pace as before.

At eight thirty, an hour and a half later, the boys arrived at the hospital. Since it was past visiting hours, we all had to stand outside the window of his Intensive Care room and observe Steve from the other side of the glass. It didn't feel like we were looking at Steve, my husband and their father. It felt so unnatural. ❀

The boys spent the night next to me in the waiting room. And, for the first time since our drive to Evansville at 3:53 that morning, I felt like Steve was right next to me. Through his children.

LUKE: Looking through the glass, it looked like Dad was being held up by wires and cords. It was as if he was plugged in. It didn't make any sense. We were all kind of shocked. We were the family that was always helping others. But now we were the ones that needed help.

TYLER: I've never seen Dad like that.

CODY: I had a lot of questions running through my mind.

1.1 HOME

by Steve Zeller

I woke up in the middle of the night to a voice, and I slowly opened my eyes.

My room was dark, but the light from the hospital hallway bled into my room through the cracks of the door. Tubes and wires seemed to entangle me, as if a hundred arms were holding me down. All was quiet—except for the steady beeping of the heart equipment next to my bed.

Beep. Beep. Beep.

I tiredly scanned the room, searching for this "voice" I heard, as I lay motionless in my bed. For the past four days, it felt like every time I awakened I was slowly peeling past cobwebs in my mind. I had no idea what was going on. Everything was unclear. The evening of my surgery, I vaguely remember seeing Cody standing over my bed and thinking to myself, "Oh no, he's going to pull the plug." I even wondered if that was a dream.

I gave up scanning the room. The slightest movement, even something as small as turning my head, was uncomfortable and painful. Every thirty minutes, every day, a nurse or family member would help turn my body over in an effort to help me find a comfortable position. I might feel content for a minute or two, but then the pain and discomfort would return. Sleeping was my only antidote for the pain.

My eyes heavily began to shut again when I heard the voice once more.

I wearily opened my eyes.

Beep. Beep. Beep.

I noticed the shadows on the walls.

My eyelids once again fell, and I once again heard the voice.

I groggily opened my eyes.

Beep. Beep. Beep.

I thought I might be dreaming.

What was I hearing? What was going on?

I finally looked down.

That's when I noticed Luke's six foot eleven frame kneeling next to my bed. His eyes were closed, his elbows were resting on my bed, and his hands were cupped together. ✵

"God," I heard him say, "would you reach down and touch Dad with Your healing hand?"

✵

LUKE: The days following Dad's surgery had been bizarre. I had never seen him that weak before. He couldn't walk to the bathroom on his own, so we had to hold him and guide him. He couldn't sleep on his back because it hurt his chest, so he had to sleep on his side as we wedged at least ten pillows up against his back. We even had to help him with breathing exercises. I felt like all I could do was pray. The strongest place I could be was on my knees, at the foot of the cross, praying for Dad.

There, in one of my weakest moments, was my proudest moment as a father. Here was my son asking God to help me.

I once again thought about Dave Manzer's prayer: *Steve knows that the hands that will touch him both physically and spiritually are Your hands.* The hands clasped together on my bedside, Luke's hands, were also God's hands.

This is one of the most mysterious, wondrous concepts to this life—that we can experience God through one another, that He can live in us and through us, thus making relationships even more important in this lifetime.

Everything had come full circle.

I remembered when my own father went to Rochester, Minnesota, to repair his brain aneurysm when I was a child, and I had, for the first time, offered an intimate prayer up to God, as I climbed down from the top of my bunk bed and knelt in the middle of our bedroom in my underwear. It was the first time I ever depended on God—there, as a nine-year-old boy—and here I was, watching my son depend on God in that exact same way.

Moments such as this, when I wake up in the middle of the night to find my oldest son praying over me while he thinks I'm asleep, I'm reminded that God has been guiding me all along, and, at times, carrying me. As Mary Stevenson's famous "Footprints in the Sand" poem concludes, "The Lord replied, 'The times when you have seen only one set of footprints, is when I carried you.'"

After that experience with Luke praying next to my bed, I had a renewed outlook on life. Days before, I had apparently experienced something close to what we know as "death," but days later, I was reminded of true "life" as heaven fell upon my hospital room.

I realized on a whole new level that God cared about me, not just because I lived, but because He met me right where I was, because He allowed me to experience this moment. He carried me, just as He carried Lorri days before when Luke, Tyler, and Cody showed up at the hospital the day of my surgery.

He carried us through our children.

Over time, that experience with Luke caused me to take a step back and reflect on our story as a family and how God had been guiding us and carrying us all along. From Iowa (where Luke was born), to California (where Tyler was born), to Minnesota (where Cody was born), and to Indiana where we just so happened to establish our roots in a tiny community that was absolutely entrenched in basketball—what are the chances?

And yet, today, as I reflect on my family, it's not our children's State championships, Mr. Basketball awards, college accolades, or NBA contracts that make me the most proud. It was moments like these—when Luke was praying at my bedside, or when Tyler thanked us for teaching him to value academics over athletics upon receiving his Academic All-American award, or when Cody told ESPN how he valued saving his money after his first NBA contract rather than making an elaborate purchase—that made me the most proud as a father.

It has always been about something bigger, something more long-lasting than championships and awards, something that transcends all the little things this world has to offer. Teaching our children to believe in something that was bigger than themselves freed them from the pressures of a world that, in a way, thought much too big of them because they played a sport. Parenting must be bigger than sports and performance. Parenting must be bigger than you.

A journalist once ran through the list of our boys' accomplishments and then asked me, "What's the greatest thing you've ever done in your life?"

I immediately responded, "I haven't done it yet."

He looked at me, as if to say, "Look at all that your boys have accomplished, and you're going to brush over it all?"

I really do believe the greatest thing we will ever do is spend eternity with Jesus. The in-between is a wonderful journey and adventure, filled with splashes of heaven along the way, filled with beautiful relationships as we walk alongside one another, and this can feel a bit like home, but this world is not our family's destination—it's not our home. That would be an existence that is far too small.

***

Following my surgery in 2007, I felt like I had been given a second chance at life. If I had been born in a different time, I wouldn't have been able to have the operation that I had. I would have eventually died of heart complications. Even in our modern age, I apparently barely survived it. ✸

LUKE: I could tell that Dad had a renewed outlook on life and his faith after his surgery. Dad has always been one to seize each moment and enjoy each experience, but after his surgery, it was even more so. It was like Dad went from acknowledging God to walking with Him.

TYLER: It just seemed like he wanted to soak life up any way he could.

CODY: He had a fresh heart, but he still couldn't beat us in basketball.

These were bonus years, I felt. I had a whole new life ahead of me after nearly losing the one I had. Each time I heard Tim McGraw's song, "Live Like You Were Dying," it felt as if the song had been written for me.

The year after my surgery, Luke graduated from Notre Dame and started a non-profit basketball ministry called DistinXion that hosted basketball camps around the state of Indiana in an effort to teach character through sports—just as he had always envisioned on our car rides to Fort Wayne during his AAU days. That is, once I stopped chewing him out.

Around this time, I also began to feel somewhat restless at Perdue Foods and believe it might be time for a change. I truly enjoyed managing the plant, but I had also been there for twenty years, and felt like I wanted to pursue something different with this fresh perspective on life that I had since my surgery.

Lorri, too, began to have the same feelings working in the athletic department at Washington High School. We both loved our jobs and we especially loved the people, but we also knew that, in the blink of an eye, all of our boys would have their college degrees and their entire lives ahead of them. We had never really thought about retirement because we both enjoyed working and the people we were working with.

Lorri and I talked it over, and we decided that nothing on this earth could be more meaningful than investing in something that our children were passionate about. And we started to explore whether we could ever work full-time with Luke's basketball ministry, DistinXion. We decided it might be a leap of faith, but we could map out a plan and do so. We decided to pursue it.

I guess you could say that we wanted to continue to influence children, even if they were someone else's children.

Because DistinXion hosted most of its camps in the summer, it gave Luke the opportunity to continue pursuing his dream of one day playing in the NBA while he managed his non-profit ministry in his summer offseason.

Luke played professional basketball in Japan and Lithuania before getting drafted into the NBA D-League by a feeder team for the San Antonio Spurs. He secured an NBA contract when he played for the Phoenix Suns during the 2012-13 season. He fulfilled his dream, and it's pretty cool to say that all three of our boys played in the NBA.

It would have been extremely easy for him to give up. His route to the NBA was certainly unconventional. But he kept persevering. He kept pushing. He set his eyes on something and decided he wasn't going to give up until he achieved it or until he was forced away from the game. ❖

Over the years, DistinXion has continued to subtly grow, and Luke and his wife, Hope, spend much of their time and energy pouring themselves into the ministry. Today, Lorri and I work for DistinXion, and Luke is our boss, technically. ❖

We can't think of anything more fulfilling than being able to witness Luke's dream in action on a day-to-day basis and take part in his vision—to come alongside him and grab his hand, like my father did that Christmas Eve of 1968 when I was six years old.

When each of my parents died, passing through this world and into the next, entering their eternal home, they included the names of

TYLER: When Luke got that contract, I was really happy for him. He worked his butt off. He went overseas. He played in the NBA D-League. I honestly don't know if I would have been able to make it through all of that. The fact that Luke did make it through says a lot about who he is as a person.

CODY: The 2012-13 season was an exciting one for me because of everything happening at IU, but seeing Luke get his contract with the Suns was probably the highlight of my year.

LUKE: They found my dream so important that they literally wanted to pour their entire lives into it.

each of their twelve children on their headstones. It was a bit bizarre to stand over their graves and see my name etched into a tombstone, but at the same time, it was a perfect representation of who they were and the lives they led. They believed their greatest gift to this world was their children, and Lorri and I share that belief.

We believe parenthood is the greatest responsibility *in* the world but also the greatest opportunity to give something *to* the world. And we would like to be remembered, not for what we did, but rather for what our children became, for what they represent, for where they are headed.

We hope and pray that our home, our family, and the Zeller name, will forever reflect a truer home—something that is bigger than sports, bigger than ourselves, and bigger than our tiny worlds—a destination, our truest calling.

ACKNOWLEDGMENTS

The chorus of Kenny Chesney's song "Never Wanted Nothing More" talks about only needing two things to be happy in life: loving and laughing. Simple as it may be, our belief is that these two things are best lived out in the context of relationships.

Recently, an elderly woman in Washington passed away, and at her funeral, her children spoke about the fact that she always taught them that "You don't love *things*; you only love *people*." Apparently, she was really strict with her children when it came to this concept. If one of them said something like, "I love chocolate," she would correct them and say, "You don't love *things*; you only love *people*."

Returning to Chesney's song, sure, you can love something on your own—your job, your possessions, yourself—but it's more meaningful to give your love *to* someone else; and sure, you can laugh on your own—perhaps while watching television or listening to a comedian's stand-up routine—but it's more enjoyable to laugh *with* someone else.

We have always believed that a primary avenue for discovering real meaning in this life is found in relationships with others—walking alongside people, shoulder to shoulder, through the highs and lows of life. Simply put, we consider ourselves blessed because of the people in our lives—yes, our children, which is what this book is about, but also all of our friends and family members who have supported us, encouraged us, and challenged us along the way.

From our roots in Iowa to the many years we have spent in Indiana to all the stops in between, namely California and Minnesota, we are truly thankful for everyone who has loved and laughed alongside us on the journey.

That being said, we want to extend a special "thank you" to everyone who has supported us along the way, whether you have been friends with us for decades or whether you spent your valuable time reading this book because you believe in what we stand for—faith and family. Thank you. From the bottom of our hearts. We are humbled you would even consider reading our story.

Specifically to our friends (and what we mean by friends is "family") in Washington, Indiana, the journey has been enjoyable primarily because it has been alongside all of you. Thank you.

As we have said, we don't claim to know the answers when it comes to parenting, we only claim to have learned a lot as we've lived through a story we never could have fathomed. Though there is "molding" and "shaping" that takes place in the household, we know our children would not be the young men they are today if it wasn't for the coaches, teachers, professors, teammates, teammates' parents, friends, friends' parents, and fans who have impacted them along the way. Again, thank you.

Hopefully, in some way, this book gave you a few laughs and helped you love a little more. We look forward to loving and laughing alongside all of you, all the way to the other side of eternity, when we are finally home.

by Steve and Lorri Zeller